Death
The Door to Heaven

Hushidar Hugh Motlagh

Global Perspective

**To order copies
of this book and other works
by Global Perspective, call or fax:**

989-772-1432

1-800-949-1863 (only in U.S.)

If you prefer, order online or by mail:

Website: www.globalperspective.org

Email: info@globalperspective.org

Address: Global Perspective
1106 Greenbanks Dr.
Mt. Pleasant, MI 48858
USA

Cover design by Lori Block

ISBN: 0937661384
LCCN: 2006924981

Dedicated to

*Betty Cumberland, a model of service to humankind, whose desire for spreading the knowledge of **the Glory of God** knows no bounds.*

For the earth shall be filled with the knowledge of ***the glory of the Lord***, as the waters cover the sea.

Habakkuk 2:14

In My Father's house are many mansions...I go and prepare a place for you, I will come again and receive you to Myself; that where I am, there you may be also. Christ (John 14:2-3 NKJ)

He, verily, is come with His Kingdom, and all the atoms cry aloud: '***Lo! The Lord is come in His great majesty!***'

Bahá'u'lláh

Reunion with God

Thy Paradise is My love; thy heavenly home, reunion with Me.   *Bahá'u'lláh*

In My Father's house are many mansions... I go to prepare a place for you. And if I go and prepare a place for you, I will come again and receive you to Myself; that where I am, there you may be also.
                    Christ (John 14:2-3 NKJ)

To those who do good, a good reward in this present world; but better is the mansion of the next, and splendid the abode of the God-fearing!   *Qur'án 16:30*

The dust returns to the ground...and the spirit returns to God...   *Ecclesiastes 12:7 NIV*

You guide me with your counsel, and afterward you will take me into glory. Whom have I in heaven but you?
                    Psalms 73:24-25 NIV

Contents

Part I
The Afterlife

Part II

Bahá'u'lláh
The Glory of God

Part III
Books that Can Change Your Destiny

Appendix

*A New Series
of Mini-Books
for Busy Readers*

"Blazon-His-Name" Series

Dear Seeker of Knowledge:

This is the state of the western world: "There is so much to do and so little time to do it." Many people fail to spare enough time for their families, let alone for reading a whole book on impractical and elusive subjects, such as who are we, why are we here, and what on earth are we doing? Life is too short to spend it in search of answers that may never be found.

This volume is written for those who can find a little time for their soul. It is one of a series of mini books on human purpose and destiny, written in response to the changing times.

These books will make your life a little easier in a number of ways:

These books will make your life a little easier in a number of ways:

- You are more likely to read them and feel less guilty for not reading them!

- You are more likely to share them with friends, and feel less disappointed for knowing that they are neither reading them nor have any intention of returning them to you!

- You are saved from the agony of buying and keeping a large book you may not like.

- You can begin with a subject that interests you.

What purpose do these mini books serve? Their prime purpose is:

- To inspire you to investigate "the Greatest and Most Joyous News" the world has ever known: the glorious News of the Advent of the promised Redeemer of our time, Bahá'u'lláh, the Glory of God.

- To give you a taste of some of Bahá'u'lláh's teachings and to describe briefly God's plan for each of us and for the world.

Since this copy may be the first and the last one you may ever receive, a brief introduction to Bahá'u'lláh's life and a list of suggested readings, are included at the end of most volumes. Please send your comments and suggestions to the author:

hugh@globalperspective.org

Time does not wait for anyone. We must choose our destiny, or "the relentless course of events" will make all the choices for us.

True wisdom lies in gathering the precious things out of each day as it goes by.

Books in This Series

Knowing and Loving God

1. *Do You Really Know Who You Are?* The glory and the joy of knowing yourself

2. *God's 19 Great Little Tranquilizers.* Heaven's prescription for peace and tranquility

3. *Seize Your Chance*. Destiny is a choice. Have you made yours?

4. *Prayer: The Key that Unlocks the Heart of Heaven*

5. *Death: The Door to Mansions of Heaven*

6. *Did God Create the Universe, or is it an Accident?*

7. *Why Suffer? Take Heaven's Advice.* Learning to understand and cope with adversity

Death
The Door to Heaven

Hushidar Hugh Motlagh

Preface

Why did we come into this world? Did we come to live for a few decades and then disappear into a grave? No! This book shows that we are here for a purpose—a most glorious purpose. We are at the beginning of an everlasting journey, where we pause for a moment, and then move on. Yet that one moment matters more than the eternity that follows it. It sets the course for the rest of our journey. The choices we make in this world determine our destiny in all the worlds that follow it. Should we not then learn how to spend this one moment the way God would wish us to spend it?

What a waste of the precious gift of life to live without knowing why we are here, where we are going, and how we can reach our destination—the one God has chosen for us. This small book offers the signposts that can help us make our journey pleasant and fruitful not only during our brief stay here, but also during the eternity that follows it.

Part I

The Afterlife

1

Unto God
Shall We Return

Reunion with God

Sacred Scriptures declare that we are God's and unto Him shall we return:

> "Behold, all souls are Mine" (Eze.18:4). "In God's hand are...the spirits of all human kind" (Job 12:10 NEB). "At death, God takes souls unto Himself" (Qur'án 39:43). "I saw the souls of those that were beheaded for the witness of Jesus" (Rev. 20:4). "The spirit shall return unto God" (Eccl. 12:7). "Unto Him shall all return"[1] (the Báb). "Hereafter shall you return to your Lord, and He will tell you of your works" (Qur'án 39:9). "As from a fire aflame thousands of sparks

come forth, even so from the Creator an infinity of being have [received] life and to Him return again..." (Upanishad). "Verily, we are God's... And unto Him we do return"[2] (Bahá'u'lláh).

Is it not nice to know that for homecoming we will all return to God? We see death as evil; God sees death as good:

> I have made death a messenger of joy to thee. Wherefore dost thou grieve?[3]   Bahá'u'lláh

> The spirit of holiness beareth unto thee the joyful tidings of reunion; wherefore dost thou grieve?[4]   Bahá'u'lláh

> Rejoice, for the eternal life is awaiting you.[5]
> 'Abdu'l-Bahá

> Be faithful, even to the point of death, and I will give you the crown of life.   Rev. 2:10 NIV

We are not the permanent residents of this planet, but travelers on a voyage to a new and exciting world:

> Everything that man does, every experience that he encounters, his whole world, mental and physical, is there for but one purpose—to launch him on an eternal voyage to a destination far better than his dearest dreams.[6]

Can a question in human life matter as much as this: is death a voyage to the grave or to God? Is death "extinguishing the light, or quenching the lamp because the sun hath risen"? The question is vital, indeed urgent, because our stay on the earth, compared to eternity, is very brief. It counts even less than a moment.[7] Yet that moment may matter more in determining our final destiny than the eternity that follows it. Hence any time spent in unraveling the mystery of death and immortality is time well spent.

> Remember Him before the silver cord is snapped and the golden bowl is broken, before the pitcher is shattered...before the dust returns to the earth as it began and the spirit returns to God who gave it.
> Eccl. 12:6-7 NEB

> Life is real! Life is earnest!
> And the grave is not its goal;
> Dust thou art, to dust returnest,
> was not spoken of the soul.

"There was a famous king in history who appointed a man to live in his royal presence and to say every day to him, 'Philip, remember thou art mortal,' lest he forget his kinship with the earth. But doesn't every person need another daily whisper in his ears, 'Remember, thou art immortal,' lest he forget his kinship with eternity?"

What are we? An everlasting soul or billions of dying cells? As noted psychologist, Dr. Wayne Dyer observes:

> I see my form changing all the time. If I thought that was all that I am, I would feel distressed over my physical changes. But I know that I am much more than this form that I occupy. *I know that I am a soul with a body, rather than a body with a soul.*[8]

The Báb declares that here we live in a dream. At death, we wake up from the dream. This is an illusive life, the next an awakened life. As dreams are mostly illusions, so are many of our assumptions, fears, and beliefs, such as our concern for the decline of our physical form.

Is this life the beginning or the end of a journey? Does the drama of human life terminate here in this world? Bahá'u'lláh reaffirms and restates repeatedly the immortality of the human soul:

> O SON OF MAN!
> Thou art My dominion and My dominion perisheth not, wherefore fearest thou thy perishing? Thou art My light and My light shall never be extinguished, why dost thou dread extinction? Thou art My glory and My glory fadeth not; thou art My robe and My robe shall never be outworn. Abide then in thy love for Me, that thou mayest find Me in the realm of glory.[9]

We are God's Love made visible; His Wisdom displayed; His Knowledge laid bare; His Thoughts and Attributes unveiled to the fullest.

> How resplendent the luminaries of knowledge that shine in an atom, and how vast the oceans of wisdom that surge within a drop! To a supreme degree is this true of man, who, among all created things, hath been invested with the robe of such gifts, and hath been singled out for the glory of such distinction. For in him are potentially revealed all the attributes and names of God to a degree that no other created being hath excelled

or surpassed. All these names and attributes are applicable to him. Even as He hath said: "Man is My mystery, and I am his mystery."[10]

Bahá'u'lláh

It is contrary to the Wisdom of the all-knowing to efface His most beloved creation, a being so sublime as to mirror forth the Creator Himself. God destroying us is like a lover destroying his best-beloved, a viewer desecrating his own image, a genius undoing his master work. It is as though God has rejected part of His own Self. What is the worth of a human if he can be buried in a grave?

That which possesses the body is eternal. It cannot be limited or destroyed.   Bhagavad-Gita

It is sown a natural body, it is raised a spiritual body.   I Cor. 15:44

All human beings need a vision of the future. Without it, life turns into a journey of despair. Eternity is a seed planted in every soul (Eccl. 3:11). Our vision of the future is the sunshine that nourishes the seed, that allows the "eternity" to blossom forth and flourish. The death of the seed is the death of hope.

There is a God-shaped vacuum in every heart.

Blaise Pascal

Evidence for the Afterlife

If our life were to end here, why would God's great Messengers and Teachers—the essence and the

source of all Knowledge and all Wisdom—consent
to bear the unbearable: rejection, ridicule, torture,
and death? Consider the following statement from
Bahá'u'lláh:

> How could such Souls have consented to sur-
> render themselves unto their enemies if they
> believed all the worlds of God to have been re-
> duced to this earthly life? Would they have will-
> ingly suffered such afflictions and torments as
> no man hath ever experienced or witnessed?[11]

A most evident sign of the spirit is revealed to us
in the dream world. What is it, we might ask, that
can soar without wings, see without sight, hear
without sound, converse without words?

> Sleep and death—they differ in duration rather
> than in quality. Perhaps both are sojourns in the
> spiritual, the real world. In one case our carriage
> waits nightly to take us back from the entrance
> of slumber, while in the other, having arrived at
> our destination and with no further use for the
> carriage, it is dismissed.[12]

What is the power in us that can leap into the future,
unravel the unknown, and unfold mysteries as yet
unborn? The dream world is a spiritual world not
confined by time and space. The fact that we sometimes dream of an event and years later observe
with wonder and awe its realization—with every
detail exactly as dreamed—indicates that the world
in which we encounter the event must be an independent world (can exist on its own), and that we
can be a part of it and have the potential to perceive

it. What more evidence can we expect? Of course there are many other evidences, but few seem as personal and as close to our heart. In the following passage, Bahá'u'lláh refers to the dream world as evidence of the independent existence of the soul:

Consider thy state when asleep. Verily, I say, this phenomenon is the most mysterious of the signs of God amongst men, were they to ponder it in their hearts. Behold how the thing which thou hast seen in thy dream is, after a considerable lapse of time, fully realized. Had the world in which thou didst find thyself in thy dream been identical with the world in which thou livest, it would have been necessary for the event occurring in that dream to have transpired in this world at the very moment of its occurrence. Were it so, you yourself would have borne witness unto it. This being not the case, however, it must necessarily follow that the world in which thou livest is different and apart from that which thou hast experienced in thy dream. This latter world hath neither beginning nor end. It would be true if thou wert to contend that this same world is, as decreed by the All-Glorious and Almighty God, within thy proper self and is wrapped up within thee. It would equally be true to maintain that thy spirit, having transcended the limitations of sleep and having stripped itself of all earthly attachment, hath, by the act of God, been made to traverse a realm which lieth hidden in the innermost reality of this world.[13]

God guides us and communicates with us through dreams and visions, often veiled by "symbols" with none or few words.

> "It is not for man that God should speak with him but by vision, or from behind a veil" (Qur'án 42:50). "God taketh souls unto Himself...during sleep...Herein are signs for the reflecting" (Qur'án 39:43). "Thus God showeth you His signs that ye may ponder on this present world, and on the next" (Qur'án 2:217-218).

All these signs, and others, point to an entity or essence independent and exalted, one transcending the bounds of time and space.

Science teaches us that nothing in nature—not even the tiniest particle—can disappear without a trace. Nature does not know extinction. All it knows is transformation. As noted scientist Von Braun indicates:

> Now, if God applies this fundamental principle to the most minute and insignificant parts of His universe, doesn't it make sense to assume that He applies it also to the human soul? I think it does. And everything science has taught me—and continues to teach me—strengthens my belief in the continuity of our spiritual existence after death. Nothing disappears without a trace.[14]

The study of near-death vision (NDV) by eminent scientists has opened a new door to the enchanting dimension of the afterlife. Scientists and scholars of various persuasions (physicians, physicists, psychologists, and philosophers) who began their search as skeptics were forced, by their own admission, to submit to their findings, to succumb to the overwhelming evidence pointing to human survival. As Dr. Raymond Moody, Dr. Melvin Morse, Dr. Michael Sabom, Dr. Kenneth Ring, and others have maintained, no explanation save the survival of human consciousness can resolve all the issues connected with near-death visions. The following two cases, out of thousands that have been studied, demonstrate the point:

> On Long Island, a seventy-year-old woman who had been blind since the age of eighteen was able to describe in vivid detail what was happening around her as doctors resuscitated her after a heart attack.
>
> Not only could she describe what the instruments used looked like, but she could even describe their colors. The most amazing thing about this to me was that most of these instruments weren't even thought of over fifty years ago when she could last see. On top of all this, she was even able to tell the doctor that he was wearing a blue suit when he began the resuscitation.[15]
>
> Another amazing case...was relayed to me by a doctor in South Dakota. Driving into the hospital one morning, he had rear-ended a car. It had been very upsetting to him. He was very worried that the people he had hit would claim neck injury and sue him for a large sum of money.

This accident left him distraught and was very much on his mind later that morning when he rushed to the emergency room to resuscitate a person who was having a cardiac arrest.

The next day, the man he had rescued told him a remarkable story: "While you were working on me, I left my body and watched you work."

The doctor began to ask questions about what the man had seen and was amazed at the accuracy of his description. In precise detail, he told the doctor how the instruments looked and even in what order they were used. He described the colors of the equipment, shapes, and even settings of dials on the machines.

But what finally convinced this young cardiologist that the man's experience was genuine was when he said, "Doctor, I could tell that you were worried about that accident. But there isn't any reason to be worried about things like that. You give your time to other people. Nobody is going to hurt you."

Not only had this patient picked up on the physical details of his surroundings, he had also read the doctor's mind.[16]

Despite all the research done and the evidence uncovered, many still remain unconcerned or unconvinced. Some people must "die" to believe in their own immortality. No wonder Jesus said:

When the Son of Man comes, will he find faith on earth?   Christ (Luke 18:8 NEB)

On the heel of a stressful winter comes the stirrings of a new life in the spring. Similarly, the stress and distress of our lives sometimes leads our hearts heavenward, and stirs in us thoughts of the greater beyond. We discover within the seed of our soul the gift of immortality.

> But there comes a moment when man wearies of the things he has won; when he suspects with bewilderment and dismay that there is some profound and eternal purpose in his being. It is then that he discovers that beyond the kingdom of the world there exists a kingdom of the soul.[17]

> I am fully convinced that the soul is indestructible, and that its activities will continue through eternity. It is like the sun, which, to our eyes, seems to set in night; but it has really gone to diffuse its light elsewhere.[18]

> Death is the opening of a more subtle life. In the flower, it sets free the perfume; in the chrysalis, the butterfly; in man, the soul.[19]

A Glimpse Into the Next Life

Bahá'u'lláh declares that there are many other worlds beyond this world, and that our earthly life is but the first step along the path of our spiritual journey—a journey that will endure for all eternity. While on the earthly plane, the voyager is unable to see beyond the boundaries of his vision, unable to discern the succeeding realms rising in magnificent glory and splendor. But lack of this perception is no proof that nothing exists beyond his vision. Even as a fetus, we are bound to the womb of the earth. Not until the barrier of birth into the new life is lifted are we in a position to view our eternal destiny.

> All I have seen teaches me to trust the Creator for all I have not seen.   Emerson

> Faith declares what the senses do not see, but not the contrary of what they see. It is above them, not contrary to them.   Blaise Pascal

> There is a limit where the intellect fails and breaks down, and this limit is where the questions concerning God, and freewill, and immortality arise.   Immanuel Kant

The knowledge of the next life is placed beyond our perception, beyond our vision. All we can discern during our earthly journey is the evidence of the next life, and all we can receive is an occasional glimpse of what is to come, without ever being able, or allowed, to see the full Panorama.

"The angels conceal from us the beauty beyond death, that we may endure life." Bahá'u'lláh declares that if we could ever lift the veil, if we could ever see the full splendor concealed from our eyes, we would become so enraptured with our vision as to lose touch with the world, and become incapable of pursuing our earthly life. Here are His words:

> Glorified art Thou, O Lord my God! Thou hast, in Thine all highest Paradise, assigned unto Thy

servants such stations that if any one of them were to be unveiled to men's eyes all who are in heaven and all who are on earth would be dumbfounded. By Thy might! Were kings to witness so great a glory they would, assuredly, rid themselves of their dominions and cleave to such of their subjects as have entered beneath the shadow of Thine immeasurable mercy and sought the shelter of Thine all-glorious name.[20]

I swear by the righteousness of God! Were anyone apprised of that which is veiled from the eyes of men, he would become so enraptured as to wing his flight unto God, the Lord of all that hath been and shall be.[21]

Scientific studies of near-death vision by such renowned figures as Dr. Kübler Ross and Dr. Raymond Moody portray death as a door to a realm filled with beauty and splendor. This is how a child described her "death:"

All I remember was waking up in a garden filled with large flowers...I looked around and saw this being. The garden was beautiful, but everything paled in his presence. I felt completely loved and nourished by his presence. It was the most delightful feeling I've ever known.[22]

A few more descriptions:

What happens after death is so unspeakably glorious that our imaginations and our feelings do not suffice to form even an approximate conception of it...

No one should fear death. I know, because I have come face to face with death several times. It is really a pleasant experience. You seem to hear beautiful music and everything is mellow and sweet and serene—no struggle, no terror, just calmness and beauty. When death comes, you will find it to be one of the easiest and most blissful experiences you have ever had.[23]

Another reason we should not know what lies beyond is that such a knowledge would infringe on our freedom of choice. We would be so overwhelmed by our heavenly vision as to be utterly subdued by intense feelings. We would be unwittingly forced to live by the Law out of no other motive than fear and hope—to avoid the punishment, and to gain the reward. We would live like a servant under the sway of an absolute master with no freedom to be his own self.

Good Deed is Its Own Reward

We know God is just, and consequently He does not, and would not, regard good and bad as equal. We also know that each act meets with a consequence—either reward or punishment. But this knowledge, Bahá'u'lláh teaches, should not be the reason for wishing to be noble, the motive for honoring and living the law. The only motive, the only reason for living a noble life should be the love of God. Even as a true lover should we aspire to love the law and live the law.

A person may be called upon to make a sacrifice, to embark on a heroic act such as saving a child from a ravaging fire. He responds to the call by plunging into the fire out of pure love for the life of the child. Before plunging, he may know that his heroism will bring honors and glories, but that is in no way the cause, or the purpose, of his heroism. He seeks and finds the reward only in the act itself. Such should be our acts of devotion and our motivation for honoring the law. Bahá'u'lláh reminds us that:

> For every act performed there shall be a recompense according to the estimate of God...For surely if deeds were not rewarded and yielded no fruit, then the Cause of God—exalted is He—would prove futile...However, unto them that are rid of all attachments a deed is, verily, its own reward.[24]

As our love for God and truth increases, our fear decreases:

> Love is a light that never dwelleth in a heart possessed by fear.[25]   Bahá'u'lláh

> There is no fear in love.   I John 4:18 NIV

In relation to the next life, the rewards are so lofty and so lasting—everlasting—and the losses so consequential that if we ever fully recognized them, we would not dare deviate from the Law—never wish to be anything but a perfect robot. In the light of that knowledge, our love for God would be utterly overwhelmed by our love for His reward, and totally crushed by our fear of the imminent punishment. In such a context, no unselfish or devoted act could ever spring from our conscience.

God in His boundless Wisdom has always provided, through His great Messengers and Redeemers, the essential knowledge about our future destiny. This knowledge remained quite unchanged during the past ages, throughout the whole span of recorded history—unchanged until Bahá'u'lláh's advent. For through Him—"the Spirit of Truth who will guide you unto all Truth"—the knowledge suddenly surged up, reflecting the uniqueness of the new age and our increased capacity. But even now it is bestowed only in preordained measures. Because as knowledge increases, freedom decreases. It is God's will that we should trust His words and live as if His words about our future destiny are absolute truth—which they are. Trusting is a test of our love for our Creator. With full knowledge, trust would have no independent existence:

> Now faith is being sure of what we hope for and certain of what we do not see.   Hebrews 11:1 NIV

This Life is a Test

The earth is God's crucible of testing. It is His great touchstone. Every soul is provided with a clear blueprint, and then given a choice to build its future destiny, a choice to prove itself, to make itself, to find itself, to become that which it deserves—a hut or a castle, a rose or a thistle.

A person with a closed mind disregards the divine blueprint, rejects the evidence, and denies the truth. He will get what he deserves. He will deprive himself of the incomparable joy and supreme honor of knowing and loving the truth, both in this world and the next. A person with an open and seeking mind examines the evidence objectively and judges fairly. He will also get what he deserves: the joy of knowing and loving the truth, and the rewards that follow both in this world and the next. The same law prevails in every other aspect of human life. Why should it differ in our relation to our Creator?

Every decision or choice we encounter is a test. Our response to the test reveals the quality of our character—brings to light what is hidden in our soul.

> We will certainly put you to the test in order to distinguish those among you who strive and steadfastly persevere. Qur'án 47:31

> Verily, God will bring everything to light, though it were but the weight of a grain of mustard-seed, and hidden in a rock or in the heavens or in the earth; for God is Subtile, informed of all.[26] Bahá'u'lláh

> For there is nothing hidden that will not be disclosed, and nothing concealed that will not be known or brought out into the open.
> Christ (Luke 8:18)

> O SON OF BEING!
> Busy not thyself with this world, for with fire We test the gold, and with gold We test Our servants.[27] Bahá'u'lláh

Trust in God reveals our "knowledge of God." It is a test of our spiritual maturity. Can we truly know God, but fail to trust Him? Our inability to have absolute faith in our Creator points to a lack of true knowledge.

A farmer shows his trust in Nature by burying his seeds in the ground. He knows that he will be repaid many times over in due season. Do we not have as much trust in God Himself as we have in His "Nature" in His Handiwork? How far from His Justice not to repay us for trusting Him, not to reward us for loving Him, for abiding by His Will, for honoring His Law:

> The reward of no good deed is or ever will be lost.[28]   Bahá'u'lláh

> And everyone who has left houses or brothers or sisters or father or mother or children or fields for my sake will receive a hundred times as much and will inherit eternal life.
> Christ (Matt. 19:29 NIV)

> The source of all good is trust in God, submission unto His command, and contentment with His holy will and pleasure.[29]   Bahá'u'lláh

A farmer who refuses to trust Nature's wisdom, who fails to cultivate and seed his farm in the springtime, has no choice but to anticipate and encounter only weeds, no choice but to labor in the cold—when Nature is in rest and in wrath—with little rewards to come, no choice but to regret his failure, to wish it were spring again. This is justice.

Whoever plants a seed beneath the sod,
And waits to see it push away the clod,
He trusts in God.
Whoever says, when clouds are in the sky,
Be patient, heart, light breaketh by and by,
Trusts the Most High.   John Tyndall

Glories of the Next Life

Let us now get a glimpse of our future destiny, of
our heavenly Home where our true essence will be
made manifest. In the following words Bahá'u'lláh
briefly lifts the veil of concealment, and reveals
glimpses of the splendors of the life to come in the
most majestic and moving terms:

Know thou of a truth that the soul, after its separation from the body, will continue to progress
until it attaineth the presence of God, in a state
and condition which neither the revolution of
ages and centuries, nor the changes and chances
of this world, can alter. It will endure as long as
the Kingdom of God, His sovereignty, His dominion and power will endure. It will manifest
the signs of God and His attributes, and will
reveal His loving-kindness and bounty. The move-
ment of My Pen is stilled when it attempteth to
befittingly describe the loftiness and glory of so
exalted a station. The honor with which the
Hand of Mercy will invest the soul is such as
no tongue can adequately reveal, nor any other
earthly agency describe.

Blessed is the soul which, at the hour of its separation from the body, is sanctified from the vain imaginings of the peoples of the world. Such a soul liveth and moveth in accordance with the Will of its Creator, and entereth the all-highest Paradise. The Maids of Heaven, inmates of the loftiest mansions, will circle around it, and the Prophets of God and His chosen ones will seek its companionship. With them that soul will freely converse, and will recount unto them that which it hath been made to endure in the path of God, the Lord of all worlds. If any man be told that which hath been ordained for such a soul in the worlds of God, the Lord of the throne on high and of earth below, his whole being will instantly blaze out in his great longing to attain that most exalted, that sanctified and resplendent station...The nature of the soul after death can never be described, nor is it meet and permissible to reveal its whole character to the eyes of men.

The Prophets and Messengers of God have been sent down for the sole purpose of guiding mankind to the straight Path of Truth. The purpose underlying Their revelation hath been to educate all men, that they may, at the hour of death, ascend, in the utmost purity and sanctity and with absolute detachment, to the throne of the Most High. The light which these souls radiate is responsible for the progress of the world and the advancement of its peoples. They are like unto leaven which leaveneth the world of being, and constitute the animating force through which the arts and wonders of the world are made manifest. Through them the clouds rain their bounty upon men, and the earth bringeth forth its fruits. All things must needs have a cause, a motive power, an animating principle. These souls and symbols of detachment have provided, and will continue to provide, the supreme moving impulse in the world of being.

The world beyond is as different from this world as this world is different from that of the child while still in the womb of its mother. When the soul attaineth the Presence of God, it will assume the form that best befitteth its immortality and is worthy of its celestial habitation.[30]

No Act Ever Lost or Effaced

"A law of nature rules that energy cannot be destroyed. You change its form from coal to steam, from steam to power in the turbine, but you do not destroy energy. In the same way, another law governs human activity and rules that honest effort cannot be lost, but that some day the proper benefits will be forthcoming."[31]

Our spiritual evolution continues endlessly; it endures as long as the Creator Himself. The perfections gained in this world are carried into the next. Following its departure from the earthly plane, the soul continues its ever-advancing journey toward its ultimate Object and Fashioner, the Impulse and the Essence of all creation. No soul is ever destroyed; no noble or ignoble thought or deed ever fades or is forgotten. Nothing can ever be done without lasting consequences, without being engraved on imperishable and unfading tablets—the conscience of creation—there to endure throughout all eternity. As Bahá'u'lláh states:

> Every act ye meditate is as clear to Him as is that act when already accomplished. There is none other God besides Him. His is all creation and its empire. All stands revealed before Him; all is recorded in His holy and hidden Tablets.[32]

> ...I [God] behold your actions...   Qur'án 34:10

Our life consists of tiny seconds and "little" caring or uncaring acts. Seldom are we called upon to take giant leaps or engage in grand adventures. Thus it is the accumulation of little acts that ultimately count the most. This idea is confirmed by Dr. Moody in *The Light Beyond*:

> It was those kinds of things—the little things you do while not even thinking—that come up most importantly in the review [of one's record of deeds].

> Many people are asked by the being, "What was in your heart while this was going on?"[33]

Every act of kindness, such as greeting a stranger or offering someone a cup of water, will count and be rewarded:

If ye are greeted with a greeting, then greet ye
with a better greeting, or at least return it; God
taketh count of all things.   Qur'án 4:88

And if anyone gives even a cup of cold water
to one of these little ones because he is my disciple, I tell you the truth, he will certainly not
lose his reward.   Christ (Matt. 10:42)

A disturbed person may "take his life" only to find
his soul in agony, like a bud suddenly crushed
open—intense, broken, regretful. A selfish soul may
blindly exult in its shrewdness, in the brief splendors of earthly life, only to find itself, upon departure from the mortal realm, bowed down by intense
guilt, by the inseparable burden of its own self. A
sinner may live a full-fledged life of sin, hoping to
find an escape at the end of the journey, only to find
himself face to face with the full panorama of his
evil acts. Alas, no escape for anyone.

O HEEDLESS ONES!
Think not the secrets of hearts are hidden, nay,
know ye of a certainty that in clear characters
they are engraved and are openly manifest in the
holy Presence.[34]   Bahá'u'lláh

The strength of the divine Law in cultivating and
controlling the human conscience springs from this:
that one may escape the dictates of his country, but
not those of his conscience; that one can elude his
society, but not his own self; that one can evade
human punishment, but not the divine punishment.

Mrs. Rúhíyyih Rabbání uses the following beautiful and picturesque analogy to show how the role we play here transfers to the hereafter, how the true portrait of our souls hangs on our conscience for ages to come:

> ...we take the picture in this world; the views, the colors, the subjects are all preserved on the film. Over part of it we have no choice...but over part of it we have complete sway, for we can choose our angles, our time of the day, our immediate subjects. This is what we do during our everyday life; we make the film; it is small, one little picture after another...When we die the film is projected...[Pictures] we never realized we were taking appear on the screen: down in the corner we may have got the village dump (we did not want it in—but there it is!) and in a bed of flowers we may suddenly discover butterflies hovering and glimmering about, an unexpected touch of beauty, an added joy to us now...

> We can no longer take these views over again; the time, the place, the people, are all gone. Perhaps our film will be a joy to us—we shall be rewarded for all the patient effort we put into it. Perhaps we shall find it mediocre and dull and wish we could introduce improvements. Perhaps we shall discover some horror reproduced there, a murder scene, an act of brutality, some obscenity that haunts us; we are punished perpetually by its presence. What can we do? The camera, our body, and life, our subject, are all gone.[35]

Spiritual Death

Life is not lost by dying; life is lost minute by minute...in all the thousand small uncaring ways.[36]

The righteous are called alive in death; the wicked are called dead even when alive.[37]

Bahá'u'lláh teaches that "spiritual death" signifies debasement, not extinction or destruction. When a soul is said to be dead or destroyed, having failed to attain "eternal life," it simply means that it has failed to pursue its ultimate purpose. Instead of rising it has fallen, instead of advancing it has declined—to a state of spiritual poverty in the dire depths of selfishness and remoteness from God. As 'Abdu'l-Bahá observes, the eye and the nail are both endowed with life, yet the latter functions at such a low level as to be in a state of death, in comparison with the former. Thus even the most depraved, cruel, and negligent souls will enjoy "a second chance!" They will receive further opportunities to rise, but from the lowest and dimmest point named hell.

The waters of everlasting life have, in their fullness, been proffered unto men. Every single cup hath been borne round by the hand of the Well-Beloved. Draw near, and tarry not, though it be for one short moment.[38]   Bahá'u'lláh

...free thyself from the veils of idle fancies and enter into My court, that thou mayest be fit for everlasting life and worthy to meet Me. Thus may death not come upon thee, neither weariness nor trouble.[39]   Bahá'u'lláh

Heaven and Hell

Hell is truth seen too late—duty neglected in its season.[40]

'Abdu'l-Bahá teaches that heaven and hell do not stand for places. They rather refer to states of perfection, or imperfection, attained by the soul. They represent a spectrum signifying our stage of spiritual advancement. Toward one end—hell—lies the domain of darkness, where selfish forces prevail and thrive. Toward the other end—heaven—reigns the realm of light, where purity, love, wisdom, truth and all the divine virtues mingle and merge in magnificent glory and splendor—like rainbows, intertwined, embracing the heavens.

Even on the earthly plane, such states constantly permeate and dominate our lives, for the kingdom of heaven also reigns within (Luke 17:21), deep in the soul.

How often in our everyday lives we call happiness "heaven" and say, in the depths of grief or agony, that we are in "hell." They are both inside us. We do not go to them when we die, we take them with us.[41]

Heaven will be inherited by every man who has heaven in his soul.[42]

There may be some doubt about hell beyond the grave but there is no doubt about there being one on this side of it.[43]

A cruel, selfish, and hate-ridden heart harbors hell. A pure, rich, and radiant heart dominated by love, mercy, charity, and truth is a haven of heaven, a home of paradise, a habitation of God Himself.

O SON OF DUST!

All that is in heaven and earth I have ordained for thee, except the human heart, which I have made the habitation of My beauty and glory; yet thou didst give My home and dwelling to another than Me; and whenever the manifestation of My holiness sought His own abode, a stranger found He there, and, homeless, hastened unto the sanctuary of the Beloved. Notwithstanding I have concealed thy secret and desired not thy shame.[44]   Bahá'u'lláh

Such a view of human destiny, such an abstract image of hell and heaven, represents a more advanced stage of truth. It is more fitting to our present potential and maturity, one beyond the understanding of the peoples of past ages. In the following passage Bahá'u'lláh testifies to the reality of heaven and hell both in this world and the next. He also points to the conditions conducive to their realization:

As to Paradise: It is a reality and there can be no doubt about it, and now in this world it is realized through love of Me and My good-pleasure. Whosoever attaineth unto it God will aid him in this world below, and after death He will enable him to gain admittance into Paradise whose vastness is as that of heaven and earth. Therein the Maids of glory and holiness will wait upon him in the daytime and in the night season, while the day-star of the unfading beauty of his Lord will at all times shed its radiance upon him and he will shine so brightly that no one shall bear to gaze at him. Such is the dispensation of Providence, yet the people are shut out by a grievous veil. Likewise apprehend thou the nature of hell-fire and be of them that truly believe.[45]

Daniel describes hell as "everlasting contempt" and heaven as "everlasting life" (Dan. 12:2). Christ portrays hell as "eternal punishment" and heaven as "eternal life" (Matt. 25:46).

The Báb describes paradise and the means of attaining that most glorious gift in these words:

No created thing shall ever attain its paradise unless it appeareth in its highest prescribed degree of perfection...Man's highest station, however, is attained through faith in God in every Dispensation and by acceptance of what hath been revealed by Him...[46]

For those who have been faithful to God's Covenant, death is not doom but joy and peace; it is not darkness but a crown of life, an immortal glory and honor:

Be thou faithful unto death and I will give you a crown of life.   Christ (Rev. 2:10)

> Precious in the sight of the Lord is the death of his saints.   Psalms 116:15

The death of an infant is a loss only for the occupants of this earthly kingdom. God's heavenly kingdom contains many gardens and many growing flowers. "We weep over the grave of little ones taken from us by death; but an early grave may be the shortest way to heaven." Our judgment remains faulty unless it views the world through the Vision of Providence. To a mother who had lost a son, 'Abdu'l-Bahá wrote:

> ...although the loss of a son is indeed heartbreaking and beyond the limits of human endurance, yet one who knoweth and understandeth is assured that the son hath not been lost but, rather, hath stepped from this world into another, and she will find him in the divine realm. That reunion shall be for eternity, while in this world separation is inevitable and bringeth with it a burning grief...

> That beloved child addresseth thee from the hidden world: 'O thou kind Mother, thank divine Providence that I have been freed from a small and gloomy cage and, like the birds of the meadows, have soared to the divine world—a world which is spacious, illumined, and ever gay and jubilant. Therefore, lament not, O Mother, and be not grieved; I am not of the lost, nor have I been obliterated and destroyed. I have shaken off the mortal form and have raised my banner in this spiritual world. Following this separation is everlasting companionship. Thou shalt find

me in the heaven of the Lord, immersed in an ocean of light.'[47]

Is there any pain and anguish (disease, failure, betrayal, or loss...) in the next realm? Pain and anguish hereafter comes from our failures here, from our remoteness from God, from being deprived of His glory, from remembering lost opportunities, from saying "I wish I..." "Why didn't I...?" "I could have at least..." "Why was I so...?" The memories of our spiritual stagnation here are the links of an undying "worm" that will pester our conscience hereafter for ages to come.

> ...hell...where their worm does not die...
> Christ (Mark 9:44-48 NIV)
> See also Isaiah 66:18, 22-24

Anguish can also come from seeing apathy, selfishness, negligence, and remoteness from God in our loved ones who refuse to awaken and arise while they have a chance, who decline to take their share of the heavenly bounties.

The next realm itself is not a source of afflictions and calamities:

> The eternal realm...is sanctified from all afflictions and calamities.[48]   'Abdu'l-Bahá

This is the time and here is the place where we must choose our everlasting destiny—nearness to God, or remoteness from His presence. Once we pass away from this life, we will never have this chance and this choice again:

To every thing there is a season, and a time to every purpose under the heaven...

Ecclesiastes 3:1
See also John 9:4

Seize thy chance, for it will come to thee no more.[49]

Bahá'u'lláh

God has created "the heavenly mansions" for all of us. He invites everyone to His presence, to His "court of holiness" to His everlasting Banquet:

O Son of Spirit! With the joyful tidings of light I hail thee: rejoice! To the court of holiness I summon thee; abide therein that thou mayest live in peace for evermore.[50]

Bahá'u'lláh

Our Creator wishes to grant to every human being the honor of attaining His presence in the heavenly Kingdom. And He uses every appeal conceivable to motivate and inspire us to say yes to His invitations, but he does not force us. If He did, we would no longer be human beings, we would lose the honor of reflecting His supreme image. (For examples of 15 kinds of appeals God uses to motivate us, see *Choosing Your Destiny*, Chapter 13.)

Preparation for the Next Life

I am ready to meet my maker, but whether my maker is prepared for the great ordeal of meeting me is another matter.

Winston Churchill

How can we prepare our souls for the next kingdom? By living a full and balanced life in this kingdom.

That which prepares us to live an abundant life here also prepares us to live an abundant life hereafter.

We must live in the world and soar above it as close to heaven as possible without losing touch with the earth.

> You guide me with your counsel, and afterward you will take me into glory. Whom have I in heaven but you?   Psalms 73:24-25 NIV

No lever can uplift the human soul to duty and dignity, to peace and contentment, and to strength and self-sacrifice as the hope of immortality. The most astonishing evidence of the transforming power of a firm belief in immortality comes from the change of attitude among those who attempt suicide. Studies indicate that the knowledge of the next life, as revealed through near-death visions, substantially reduces the desire for suicide.

As Dr. Raymond Moody notes:

> These results don't surprise me. Loss of hope is often the reason people try to commit suicide. They feel burdened by life and void of spiritual beliefs...Where before these people felt that life led nowhere, they now feel a rich and fulfilling afterlife awaits them. That knowledge has a way of relieving the pain in their lives. It makes them feel that life is worth living.[51]

Belief in immortality gives dignity to life and enables us to endure cheerfully those trials that come to us all. As the thought of immortality occupies our minds, we gain a clearer conception of duty and are inspired to cultivate character.[52]

Life in the hereafter is an extension of life here; it is like going from one continent to another. The desire to live in heaven inspires a desire to develop a heaven in one's soul. The heaven above builds a heaven within, and the heaven within leads to a heaven above.

There is only one way to get ready for immortality, and that is to love this life and live it as bravely and faithfully and cheerfully as we can.[53]

The earth is God's training and recruiting station for heaven. It is a school where we must learn skills that we need not only here but also after graduation. The problem is that many people ignore or repress thoughts of their graduation. They devote most of their efforts to the demands of the flesh, rather than the joys of the spirit.

Some people fear that preoccupation with hereafter undermines thoughts of living a full life here. But this concern seldom if ever is realized. The monks who separate themselves from the society may be among the few exceptions. What usually happens is just the opposite: preoccupation with living on earth undermines the realization of a full life both on earth and in heaven. In one of His Epistles Bahá'u'lláh expresses astonishment that people invest much effort into their earthly houses, which they occupy for only a short while, yet they ignore their heavenly houses, which they occupy for ever. It seems:

The wicked work harder to reach hell than the righteous strive to reach heaven.[54]

What would draw humans away from the ephemeral glamour of the present to the eternal glory of the future? Reflection is the power that dims the glamour, and meditation the light that unveils the glory.

se of life is to spend it for something life.[55]

In the early, encounter two stages and states of preparation, one physical, and the other spiritual. First begins the physical phase in the womb in the state of a seed growing limbs and roots. Then follows the spiritual seeking to manifest the fruits of the spirit. Yes, "the roots and the limbs" are left behind—cast to the winds. Only the "fruits" are kept and cast into the mold of immortality—rising out of the gloomy ashes of the ephemeral into the glorious lights of the celestial.

At death, each soul is merely the fruits of its own labors—as perfect and pure, as rich and ravishing as it has made itself.

Those who were blind in this world, will be blind in the hereafter...   Qur'án 17:72 Y

A child born into the world handicapped faces limitations and losses. A soul born into the next kingdom unprepared encounters similar consequences. Yet in both cases the limitations and losses remain unknown and unrecognized until the

voyager reaches the next stage of its journey—
where the undeveloped capacities are most needed
and their absence most evident.

The same holds true with developed capacities. The
spiritual virtues that we gain here are mostly invisible in the earthly realm. This world does not
have the capacity to reveal their full glory. We do
not and cannot appreciate their true worth until we
arrive at a spiritual realm. A diamond is invisible
in darkness, and only light can reveal its brilliance
and beauty.

A humble, pure, virtuous soul in our midst may
hold no special esteems or honors in our eyes. Only
when it casts off its crust will the wonders of its
being be made manifest.

> See that you do not look down on one of these
> little ones. For I tell you that their angels in
> heaven always see the face of my heavenly
> Father.   Christ (Matt. 18:10-11)

Despite similarities, the earthly and spiritual realms
differ in this: the consequences of the perfection or
imperfection of the fetus are temporary, for the
physical realm ends here; those of the soul are everlasting, for the spiritual life continues indefinitely.

In the context of eternity, the span of human life
on the earthly plane counts less than a moment. Yet
so many of us fail to grow in due season, in the
springtime of our journey. We fail to discern the
awesome consequences of our negligence in overcoming our imperfections. True, following our

departure from the earthly plane we will have further opportunities to evolve, to advance, but the earth is the field where the limbs and roots take form, giving rise to the final and perennial essence: the fruit. The foundation of our physical health must be laid in the womb, that of the spiritual in the womb of the earth.

Alas, the earthly splendors, the temporal glamours dim our vision; otherwise we would see and seek nothing but heavenly virtues. In the words of Bahá'u'lláh:

> Were man to appreciate the greatness of his station and the loftiness of his destiny he would manifest naught save goodly character...[56]

'Abdu'l-Bahá states that the souls who have passed on to the next Kingdom wish that they could return to the earthly home, not because of their attachment to this world but their yearning for another chance to perform noble acts of love and service, their hope to live and teach the truth. The Qur'án, too, confirms this fact:

> They will say: "Would that we were but sent back! Then would we not reject the Signs [proofs] of our Lord, but would be among those who believe."   Qur'án 6:27 Y

> Therein [in hell] they shall cry out: "Our Lord! Deliver us! We will engage in virtuous deeds, unlike what we did in the past.   Qur'án 35:37

Yet those of us who have not yet made the departure live in negligence, as though life were to end here.

We should be intelligently aware...that life is uni-directional, swift, purposeful; that we are speeding on through the days and years to a destination; at that destination we embark on a journey to a new world. We have a through ticket... and while we are carried along we must keep our wits about us and prepare what we need for that future embarkation, for we cannot keep the plane waiting and we cannot come back for anything we forget![57]

I shall pass through this world but once. Anything, therefore, that I can do, or any kindness that I can show to any human being, let me do it now. Let me not defer it or neglect it, for I shall not pass this way again![58]

A little gleam of time between two eternities; no second chance to us forever more![59]

A rich woman who had near-death vision said that for the first time she saw herself outside the context of her riches. No expensive jewelry to adorn her, no mansions to anchor her pride, no servants to serve her. Suddenly she realized that her belongings had no relevance to her. This one experience changed everything in her life.

The only thing we take with us from this world is what we are...In this world we slide through life both outwardly and inwardly with a lot of disguises...Short people wear high-heeled shoes, tall people wear low-heeled ones; clothes round out the gaps or cover the deformities; likewise, polite phrases...gloss over the poverty within...

But death strips us of these foibles. The mistaken esteem of our friends, the adulation of the foolish, the honor we possessed through appearance rather than through merit...fall away. We go as we really are into a new life.[60]

As the Scriptures teach, the Gates of the Kingdom are open only to the meek, the humble in heart, who seek and adore the truth wherever and whenever they find it.

When God arose to judgment, to save all the meek of the earth.   Psalms 76:9

For the Lord taketh pleasure in his people: he will beautify the meek with salvation.
                                                    Psalms 149:4

The spirit of the Lord God is upon me; because the Lord hath anointed me to preach good tidings unto the meek...   Isaiah 61:1

The humble are those who admit ignorance and gaze at new ideas with the wonder of a child. The humble are also those who do not place their confidence in the proud and powerful, for they know well the promise of the Scriptures that "the last shall be first, and the first last" (Matt. 20:16; Mark 10:31). What happens when the music changes and the marching band turns?

Bahá'u'lláh reminds us repeatedly of our divine essence and supreme destiny. He seeks to warn us of our accountability before our Creator, and to awaken us to "the appointed hour" that "shall inevitably come upon all of us," the hour that "none can put back." Consider the following quotations:

The generations that have gone on before you—whither are they fled? And those round whom in life circled the fairest and the loveliest of the land, where now are they? Profit by their example, O people, and be not of them that are gone astray.

Others ere long will lay hands on what ye possess, and enter into your habitations. Incline your ears to My words, and be not numbered among the foolish.

For every one of you his paramount duty is to choose for himself that on which no other may infringe and none usurp from him. Such a thing—and to this the Almighty is My witness—is the love of God, could ye but perceive it.

Build ye for yourselves such houses as the rain and floods can never destroy, which shall protect you from the changes and chances of this life. This is the instruction of Him Whom the world hath wronged and forsaken.[61]

Know ye that the world and its vanities and its embellishments shall pass away. Nothing will endure except God's Kingdom which pertaineth to none but Him, the Sovereign Lord of all, the Help in Peril, the All-Glorious, the Almighty. The days of your life shall roll away, and all the things with which ye are occupied and of which ye boast yourselves shall perish, and ye shall, most certainly, be summoned by a company of His angels to appear at the spot where the limbs of the entire creation shall be made to tremble, and the flesh of every oppressor to creep. Ye shall be asked of the things your hands have wrought in this, your vain life, and shall be repaid for your doings. This is the day that shall inevitably come upon you, the hour that none can put back. To this the Tongue of Him that speaketh the truth and is the Knower of all things hath testified.[62]

Seize the time, therefore, ere the glory of the divine springtime hath spent itself...[63]

Seize, O friends, the chance which this Day offereth you, and deprive not yourselves of the liberal effusions of His grace. I beseech God that He may graciously enable every one of you to adorn himself, in this blessed Day, with the ornament of pure and holy deeds. He, verily, doeth whatsoever He willeth.[64]

The promise of the coming of a great Redeemer at "the time of the end" is made in all the holy Scriptures (Acts 3:19-21), a Messenger destined to lead humankind not only to the earthly kingdom but to the heavenly, a divine Teacher promised to bring peace not only to the world but to the soul—leading every receptive heart to his heavenly home.

Did Jesus not speak of the many mansions in His Father's Home (John 14:2)? And did He not say to His followers "I go to prepare a place for you," and "I will come again and receive you to myself that where I am, there you may be also" (John 14:3)?

And did He not further address His followers saying that you too must prepare yourselves for receiving Me, for entering the heavenly Mansions?

> If ye choose to follow Me, I will make you heirs of My Kingdom...[65]   Bahá'u'lláh

Bahá'u'lláh proclaims, in the most certain and definitive terms, to be that same great Spirit spoken of by Jesus, that same celestial Redeemer come once again to receive us, to redeem us, and to lead us on to the heavenly Realms—the Mansions of light and glory.

Attributes Needed in the Kingdom of Heaven

As stated, this world is a school; we must work hard to graduate with honors. Failing or dropping out will be very costly. We must earn special degrees that prepare us for a smooth transfer to the heavenly schools. We need one degree that prepares us for meeting our Creator, and another that harmonizes us with His creation:

- **Klf** (Being prepared to meet God)

- **Phds** (Being in harmony with God's creation)

If you are baffled, then look at the following list and see what each degree stands for. In one of His talks, 'Abdu'l-Bahá cited seven attributes that He said would prepare us for our heavenly home:[66]

Attributes Needed in the Kingdom of Heaven

Being in Harmony with God

- *Knowledge of God* (K)

- *Love of God* (L)

- *Faith* (F)

Being in Harmony with God's Creation

- *Philanthropic deeds* (P)

- *Holiness or purity* (H)

- *Detachment* (D)

- *Self-sacrifice* (S)

The Báb and Bahá'u'lláh both place special emphasis on holiness, sanctity, and purity:

> God loveth those who are pure. Naught in the… sight of God is more loved than purity…[67]
>
> The Báb

> Possess a pure, kindly and radiant heart, that thine may be a sovereignty ancient, imperishable and everlasting.[68]   Bahá'u'lláh

> Sanctify your souls, O ye peoples of the world, that haply ye may attain that station which God hath destined for you…[69]   Bahá'u'lláh

Purity means having good motives, living honestly and sincerely, being free from deception, hypocrisy, malice, envy, lust, egotism, pretension, and pride; it means lacking a desire to manipulate or use people for one's own selfish needs and interests. Purity is the basis of other virtues. How can one know or love God if he is deceptive? How can one be charitable or engage in self-sacrifice if he is a liar, a hypocrite, or a manipulator? Little children are our best models of holiness. Their pure, pristine heart is their entrance ticket to the mansions of heaven:

> I tell you the truth, unless you change and become like little children, you will never enter the kingdom of heaven.   Christ (Matt. 18:3 NIV)

We should note that because of lack of mental growth and training, children lack wisdom. When they engage in unseemly behavior, the fault is not with their hearts but with their minds.

In an Epistle to a disciple, Bahá'u'lláh states that it is better to be an infidel than to be deceptive and cunning. A deceptive person cannot truly believe in God; and his declared faith in Providence is another deception that further adds to his hypocrisy, and puts him in a worse shape than an honest nonbeliever.

Sometimes we wish to go to the wisest person in the world and ask him for his one best advice. How wonderful it would be if we could ask this same question from the All-Wise—our Creator. Fortunately we need not remain in wonderment. Bahá'u'lláh in a very intimate letter to a disciple says that His best advice to him is to acquire the gift of a pure heart.

Those who fail to attain purity here may have to stand behind the gate of heavenly Kingdom a long, long time. If we were to hold a beautiful, fragrant banquet, would we invite a person who would spoil the beauty and purity of our feast? Would it be fair to the other invited guests to have such a person present? And even if we invited an unprepared guest, would he be comfortable at the banquet? Would he not feel ashamed in the presence of the other guests?

> Lord, who may dwell in your sanctuary? Who may live on your holy hill? He whose walk is blameless and who does what is righteous, who speaks the truth from his heart…
>
> Psalms 15:1-2 NIV

Recently I found myself in a meeting attended by a large gathering of well-dressed people listening intensely to an informative and entertaining speaker.

Suddenly, I noticed a man in working clothes sitting near me. Instantly it became evident to me that this man was out of harmony with the audience (and himself), and unable to appreciate and enjoy the talk. His mental and spiritual unpreparedness became most evident when he appeared unable to understand the speaker's humor. While the other guests were laughing and having a good time, this man was looking around with envy and anger. He occupied some of my attention, and made me uncomfortable watching his angry and bewildered face, which he kept turning around. It seemed he would be happier almost anywhere else.

By the way, I saw this man in my dream last night just after putting my finishing touches to this topic!

> Holy words and pure and goodly deeds ascend unto the heaven of celestial glory. Strive that your deeds may be cleansed from the dust of self and hypocrisy and find favor at the court of glory; for ere long the assayers of mankind shall, in the holy presence of the Adored One, accept naught but absolute virtue and deeds of stainless purity.[70]   Bahá'u'lláh

A pure heart is the shortest and surest highway to heaven. Why? Because it absorbs and reflects the truth; it radiates with love and justice and charity. Who else deserves heaven but the pure? Who else deserves to see God's glory? "Blessed are the pure in heart: for they shall see God" (Christ, Matt. 5:8). If we had a grand banquet would we invite guests with filthy clothes and foul odors? Are the banquets of heaven less worthy than those of the earth?

Should a foul soul be allowed to take a seat at the table along with the pure?

Purity is a precious prize, a divine pearl for which no effort should be spared, a heavenly gift that deserves our highest aspirations. If this pearl is missing from our hearts, then we have lived in poverty. If this gift is not found in our soul, then we have lived in vain. If this prize is not gained, we have lost the chance of a lifetime. It would be better not to have lived at all than to live and be without it.

We should note that the seed of purity grows out of self-knowledge:

> He hath known God who hath known himself.[71]
>
> Bahá'u'lláh

Where does impurity grow from? From a soil that lacks life-giving nutrients. It grows from self-deception, "vain imaginings," and "idle fancies." It arises from "pursuing empty phantoms" (Jer. 2:5), floating in the fog of fantasy, and worshiping one's own carved image of reality (Ezek. 8:12). It comes from creating and living in a dark world of illusions in which one feels comfortable with his prejudices —his selfish, immediate, and worldly needs, goals, and desires. Impurity can remain invisible only in the dark of delusion, and only true knowledge can expose it to the light.

Human beings have unlimited potential for self-deception. People who claim to be the most pious and devoted believers, torture and kill with a clear conscience the One whose name they glorify, and then call themselves heroes! If people can do this, then they can deceive themselves into doing anything that their imagination can conceive.

> There is a way that seems right to a man, but in the end leads to [spiritual] death.
>
> Proverbs 14:12 NIV

Thus the first step to purity is to break the vicious cycle of self-deception.

> Arise, O people, and, by the power of God's might, resolve to gain the victory over your own selves, that haply the whole earth may be freed and sanctified from its servitude to the gods of its idle fancies—gods that have inflicted such loss upon, and are responsible for the misery of their wretched worshippers. These idols form the obstacle that impedeth man in his efforts to advance in the path of perfection.[72]   Bahá'u'lláh

It is said that several minutes before the Titanic hit an iceberg, the radio operator received a message to this effect "This area is full of icebergs. Be careful!" His response was: "Be quiet! I am busy." Many of us sail on the sea of life with the same negligence. We are so occupied with the daily demands of life and attracted to its short-lived glamour that we lose sight of our mortality. Our Creator reminds us that while we still have time, before the iceberg has shattered our earthly dreams, we must awaken and anchor our souls on the unsinkable—the love of God. The end comes unheralded —the angel of death does not prepare us for the sudden departure:

O CHILDREN OF NEGLIGENCE!
Set not your affections on mortal sovereignty
and rejoice not therein. Ye are even as the unwary bird that with full confidence warbleth
upon the bough; till of a sudden the fowler Death
throws it upon the dust, and the melody, the form
and the color are gone, leaving not a trace.
Wherefore take heed, O bondslaves of desire![73]

Bahá'u'lláh

Why Were We Created?

Do they not reflect that God hath created the
heavens and the earth and all that is between
them for a serious end, and for a fixed term? But
truly most men believe not that they shall meet
their Lord.   Muhammad (Qur'án 30:7)

Why would have God ever wished to create us?
Did He need us? Was He lonely? God is Love,
Knowledge, Truth, Virtue, and Wisdom; and we are
the inevitable outcome of the outpouring of these
divine attributes. To be fulfilled, love must manifest
itself; it must flow unhindered, unstifled, forever
evolving, growing—unfolding its boundless charm
in myriad ways. Wisdom, knowledge, and grace
must reach out from the Source onward—to the
receivers, to the objects of Love.

But for man, who, on My earth, would remember Me, and how could My attributes and My
names be revealed?[74]   Bahá'u'lláh

O SON OF MAN!
Veiled in My immemorial being and in the ancient eternity of My essence, I knew My love for thee; therefore I created thee, have engraved on thee Mine image and revealed to thee My beauty.[75]   Bahá'u'lláh

Love without an object languishes, remains unrealized—signifying imperfection. If stillness or self-love signifies imperfection, then how can the divine Love, the essence and the fashioner of perfection, the pulse of all creation, stand hindered, stifled, still, without expression?

God stands above all needs. He is but His own Self when He unfolds His Perfections, when He unveils His Wisdom. The sun radiates not because of need, but because of its nature.

Our Ultimate Purpose and Destiny

The universe must have a purpose. The evidence of modern physics suggests strongly that the purpose includes us.[76]

To me it seems as if when God conceived the world, that was poetry; He formed it, and that was sculpture; He varied and colored it, and that was painting; and then, crowning all, He peopled it with living beings, and that was the grand divine, eternal drama.[77]

What is our ultimate purpose while on this earthly plane? If our essence is spirit, then our enduring purpose can be only spiritual, wherever or in whatever stage of our journey we may be—in this realm or the next.

The earth is God's great Touchstone, His crucible of testing. Here, the soul has almost unlimited freedom to prove its purity and sincerity. It can choose between the mortal and the immortal; between the whims of the self, and the aspirations of the spirit; between descent into the temptations of the world, and ascent to the heavenly horizons. It can cling to the earthly cage, or wing its flight to the Kingdom above; it can fall to the depths of despair and dishonor, or rise to the crest of glory and grandeur.

> ...from time immemorial even unto eternity the Almighty hath tried, and will continue to try, His servants, so that light may be distinguished from darkness, truth from falsehood, right from wrong, guidance from error, happiness from misery, and roses from thorns. Even as He hath revealed: "Do men think when they say 'We believe' they shall be let alone and not be put to proof?"[78]   Bahá'u'lláh

Our earthly life is but a seed. It is not the end, but the means to the end. The seed must sacrifice itself that it may give life to the fruit. The body must die to unfold and set free the latent powers of the spirit, for all the spiritual powers exist only as potential. The potential can bloom into the actual only by seeking, searching, and striving.

Know thou that all men have been created in the nature made by God, the Guardian, the Self-Subsisting. Unto each one hath been prescribed a pre-ordained measure, as decreed in God's mighty and guarded Tablets. All that which ye potentially possess can, however, be manifested only as a result of your own volition. Your own acts testify to this truth.[79]   Bahá'u'lláh

Without the stirrings of the divine Spirit, our potentials cannot bloom. "Human mind is a great slumbering power until awakened by a keen desire" to rise and tread the path of perfection.

Man is…the beginning of spirituality—that is to say, he is the end of imperfection and the beginning of perfection. He is at the last degree of darkness, and at the beginning of light…He has the animal side as well as the angelic side, and the aim of an educator is to so train human souls that their angelic aspect may overcome their animal side. Then if the divine power in man, which is his essential perfection, overcomes the satanic power, which is absolute imperfection, he becomes the most excellent among the creatures; but if the satanic power overcomes the divine power, he becomes the lowest of the creatures. That is why he is the end of imperfection and the beginning of perfection.[80]   'Abdu'l-Bahá

Our journey through the earthly kingdom corresponds to springtime among the seasons. If the voyager chooses to grow, to unfold, and to rise with the seasons, as the Creator has ordained, he can surely attain and fulfill his ultimate Purpose, his divine

Mission. Otherwise, he withers and falls—unful-
filled, empty, incomplete.

What is the ultimate purpose of growing, of unfolding our potential? The ultimate end is to prepare
the soul so that it may become worthy of attaining
the Presence of its Creator—the Source and Essence
of all joys, pleasures, and perfections. Our ultimate
end is nearness to God; that is our last haven, the
Object of our every hope and aspiration, our loftiest
heaven, our fondest and fairest dream, our most
enchanting and exalted happiness.

> The purpose of God in creating man hath been,
> and will ever be, to enable him to know his Cre-
> ator and to attain His Presence. To this most
> excellent aim, this supreme objective, all the
> heavenly Books and the divinely-revealed and
> weighty Scriptures unequivocally bear witness.
> Whoso hath recognized the Day Spring of Divine
> guidance [the Redeemer of the Age] and entered
> His holy court hath drawn nigh unto God and
> attained His Presence, a Presence which is the
> real Paradise, and of which the loftiest mansions
> of heaven are but a symbol.[81]   Bahá'u'lláh

Growth—or the unfolding of potentials—is the pro-
cess of rising from the self to the divine, from the
mortal to the immortal. Not to grow is a sin, a failure,
bringing its own consequence: "death" (Rom. 6:23)—
namely, stagnation of spiritual powers. Love, charity,
service, sanctity, honesty, humility, detachment
from the cares of the world, knowing, loving, and

trusting God—these are the substances on which depend the life of the spirit. In their absence, "spiritual death" dominates the soul, stifling its life-giving powers, obscuring its charm.

Let him that glorieth glory in this, that he understandeth and knoweth Me...   Jeremiah 9:24

The final test of our lives will not be how much we have lived but how we have lived, not how tempestuous our lives have been, but how much bigger, better and stronger these trials have left us. Not how much money, fame or fortune we have laid up here on earth, but how many treasure we have laid up in heaven![82]

The Link That Connects Us to God

Can you fathom the mystery of God, can you fathom the perfection of the Almighty?
                                            Job 11:7 NEB

How many are your works, O Lord! In wisdom you made them all...   Psalms 104:24 NIV

For as the heavens are higher than the earth, so are my ways higher than your ways and my thoughts than your thoughts.   Isaiah 55:9 NEB

God is our Source and our ultimate End. We stand so near to Him and yet so far from Him. We know He is infinite, beyond our vision, and utterly unknowable, yet we seek to reach Him, to know Him, and to love Him. How can the paradox be resolved?

Only if we recognize that "knowing God" means knowing His Manifestation or perfect Mirror—God made visible and knowable to man.

> The recognition of Him Who is the Bearer of divine Truth is none other than the recognition of God, and loving Him is none other than loving God.[83]   The Báb

We cannot gaze at the Sun with all its glory and splendor; we must seek its light only through mirrors—the reflectors of light. "The source of all learning," Bahá'u'lláh declares, "is the knowledge of God, exalted be His Glory, and this cannot be attained save through the knowledge of His Divine Manifestation,"[84] or His "Day Star of Truth:"

> Through the Teachings of this Day Star of Truth every man will advance and develop until he attaineth the station at which he can manifest all the potential forces with which his inmost true self hath been endowed. It is for this very purpose that in every age and dispensation the Prophets of God and His chosen Ones have appeared amongst men, and have evinced such power as is born of God and such might as only the Eternal can reveal.[85]   Bahá'u'lláh

By recognizing and obeying the mediator or the link—the Day Star of Truth—we attune our souls to the divine. We learn to guide our volition, to come into harmony with our true nature, free from impurities; we gain the strength to grow deep into the soil drawing abundant nourishment; we expand our grasp into the realm of reality—withstanding the violent winds of the self, overcoming the pains and pressures of the world.

> To know the will of God is the greatest knowledge! To do the will of God is the greatest achievement![86]

The unfolding of self, the growing of spiritual powers, result not only from striving, but also from the grace of God, reachable to us through the divine Mediators. The seed develops both by the bounties of the sun and its own strivings to grow deep in the soil. We too can unfold our potential both by the divine bounties and by our own endeavors—our pure and pious deeds. What distinguishes us from the plant is our volition: to choose death over life, hunger instead of nourishment, darkness in place of the light.

The End Is Glorious

> We have not created the heavens and the earth... save for a worthy end.   Qur'án 15:85

The course is clear, the end in sight and glorious, yet the voyager hesitates, wavers. He ignores the signs, losing sight of himself and his destiny; he stumbles and falls. He fails to discern his heavenly mission, to see his seemingly concealed self, his unending and imperishable soul. He lives as if he were the vehicle not the rider, the shell not the pearl. He builds his mansion on the earth and on sand, instead of in heaven and on his own magnificent and exalted essence—his soul. How glorious his destiny if he could rise above the barriers, if he could cherish and adore the unfading pearl concealed within the crust of his perishable passions and desires.

The Scriptures declare that our eyes should be fixed "not on the things that are seen, but on the things that are unseen: for what is seen passes away; what is unseen is eternal." (II Cor. 4:16-18; 5:1-5). The heavenly voice intimates that "flesh and blood cannot inherit the kingdom of God" (I Cor. 15:50). Yet we direct our gaze toward the seen, the ephemeral, and the earthly, losing sight of the spiritual, the unseen, the enduring, the eternal. The heavenly Voice seeks to awaken us to our supreme destiny:

O SON OF THE SUPREME!
To the eternal I call thee, yet thou dost seek that which perisheth. What hath made thee turn away from Our desire and seek thine own?[87]

Bahá'u'lláh

O MY SERVANT!
Abandon not for that which perisheth an everlasting dominion, and cast not away celestial sovereignty for a worldly desire. This is the river of everlasting life that hath flowed from the well-spring of the pen of the merciful; well is it with them that drink![88]   Bahá'u'lláh

O CHILDREN OF NEGLIGENCE!
Set not your affections on mortal sovereignty and rejoice not therein. Ye are even as the unwary bird that with full confidence warbleth upon the bough; till of a sudden the fowler Death throws it upon the dust, and the melody, the form

and the color are gone, leaving not a trace. Wherefore take heed, O bondslaves of desire![89]
Bahá'u'lláh

...set your mind upon his kingdom...Provide for yourselves never-failing treasure in heaven, where no thief can get near it, no moth destroy it.
Christ (Luke 12:31-33 NEB)

A Review of the Journey

Happy is the nation whose God is the Lord.
Psalms 33:12 NEB

Let us review briefly life's journey from its beginning to its end. We come from God, are fashioned out of love, and set on an ever-advancing yet never-ending journey toward God Himself. "We are God's, and to Him shall we return."[90]

Our immediate goal is to grow, to unfold our divine potential; our ultimate end to move toward and to attain the presence of all Perfections, God Himself.

In a sense, growing is an end in itself for it consists of the harmonizing of the self with the divine. But, ultimately, it is sought for a greater end—nearness to the Object of the endeavors. The divine in us is a perfect image concealed beneath the barrier of self, entangled in worldly attachments. The more we chisel away the unfitting and unsightly segments, the clearer the image becomes. This sums up our whole mission and purpose of living.

We can grow through love of God and through deeds springing from pure motives—self-sacrifice, detachment from the world, sanctity and holiness.

To love God we must know God, for without knowledge, love cannot take root or grow. Since God is unreachable and beyond our confined vision, we must seek to reach Him and to know Him through His Manifestations or Messengers sent to us at appointed times.

As we learn to love God by knowing Him, so do we learn to know Him by loving Him. And as we learn to live in harmony with His Will, we continue to know Him and to love Him even more. For God is Love and God is Wisdom.

To attain the fullest growth we are capable of, it is absolutely essential that we know God's latest Manifestation, the One assigned to our own age, our own dispensation.

> Man's highest station…is attained through faith in God in every Dispensation and by acceptance of what hath been revealed by Him [in the new Dispensation]…[91]   The Báb

God reveals for us in each age a new Plan and a new Purpose—more advanced, more relevant to the temper and the needs of the time. If we fail to recognize the new Plan and the new Purpose, our growth will stagnate and suffer beyond measure. We may grow, but without guidance; we may rise, but for no purpose. A person trying to grow by the teachings and the bounties of a Faith whose time has passed and whose mission is already fulfilled, is like a sapling seeking to germinate in the cold and deep shadows of darkness, or a mirror seeking light from a source that is set.

Further, by knowing and following the new Plan, our love for God continues to flourish, to abound, to evolve, to grow ever deeper and more complete. Because we can see more meaning in the new Plan, finding it more relevant to our lives, to our needs, to our nature. And, as a result of finding harmony between what we need and what we are given or asked to do, our thoughts, our ideals, our desires, and our deeds begin to move together and to harmonize, like a grand orchestra, soothing our souls and enchanting our spirits. We are no longer torn by conflicting standards and ideals; we can move confidently and contentedly in the direction of our dreams toward our ultimate destiny.

We are the signs of the knowledge of God, the radiance of His love and great glory—but the signs remain hidden in the self, the radiance is dimmed by the clouds. Only the power of sincere desire can manifest the signs, can scatter the clouds.

> From the exalted source, and out of the essence of His favor and bounty He hath entrusted every created thing with a sign of His knowledge, so that none of His creatures may be deprived of its share in expressing, each according to its capacity and rank, this knowledge. This sign is the mirror of His beauty in the world of creation. The greater the effort exerted for the refinement of this sublime and noble mirror, the more faithfully will it be made to reflect the glory of the

names and attributes of God, and reveal the wonders of His signs and knowledge.[92]

Bahá'u'lláh

Life is a divine investment. If we waste it, we displease the Investor and diminish or destroy the capital (our soul). Every 'day' must be invested for spiritual growth. A day wasted never returns; a day invested always endures.

What a loss if we misuse our cherished freedom, if we fail to fulfill our divine mission, if we lose the divine investment. We should once again hear Bahá'u'lláh's words:

O MY SERVANT!
Free thyself from the fetters of this world, and loose thy soul from the prison of self. Seize thy chance, for it will come to thee no more.[93]

Bahá'u'lláh

Dissipate not the wealth of your precious lives in the pursuit of evil and corrupt affection...[94]

Bahá'u'lláh

O friends! It behoveth you to refresh and revive your souls through the gracious favors which in this Divine, this soul-stirring Springtime are being showered upon you. The Day Star of His great glory hath shed its radiance upon you, and the clouds of His limitless grace have overshadowed you. How high the reward of him that hath not deprived himself of so great a bounty, nor failed to recognize the beauty of his Best-Beloved in this, His new attire.[95]   Bahá'u'lláh

2

Quotations from Sacred Scriptures

In My Father's house are many mansions; if it were not so, I would have told you. I go to prepare a place for you. And if I go and prepare a place for you, I will come again and receive you to Myself; that where I am, there you may be also.

Christ (John 14:2-3 NKJ)

Thy Paradise is My love; thy heavenly home, reunion with Me.[1]   Bahá'u'lláh

Death proffereth unto every confident believer the cup that is life indeed. It bestoweth joy, and is the bearer of gladness.

It conferreth the gift of everlasting life.[2]
Bahá'u'lláh

As to those that have tasted of the fruit of man's earthly existence, which is the recognition of the one true God, exalted be His glory, their life hereafter is such as We are unable to describe. The knowledge thereof is with God, alone, the Lord of all worlds.[3]
Bahá'u'lláh

The soul that hath remained faithful to the Cause of God, and stood unwaveringly firm in His Path shall, after his ascension, be possessed of such power that all the worlds which the Almighty hath created can benefit through him.[4]
Bahá'u'lláh

Bring thyself to account each day ere thou art summoned to a reckoning…[5]
Bahá'u'lláh

The world is but a show, vain and empty, a mere nothing, bearing the semblance of reality. Set not your affections upon it.[6]
Bahá'u'lláh

…the world is like the vapor in a desert, which the thirsty dreameth to be water and striveth after it with all his might, until when he cometh unto it, he findeth it to be mere illusion.[7]
Bahá'u'lláh

Busy not thyself with this world, for with fire We test the gold, and with gold We test Our servants.[8]   Bahá'u'lláh

For whoever wants to save his life will lose it, but whoever loses his life for me will find it.   Christ (Matt. 16:25 NIV)

Provide purses for yourselves that will not wear out, a treasure in heaven that will not be exhausted, where no thief comes near and no moth destroys.

Christ (Luke 12:33 NIV)

What good will it be for a man if he gains the whole world, yet forfeits his soul? Or what can a man give in exchange for his soul?   Christ (Matt. 16:26 NIV)

Do not work for food that spoils, but for food that endures to eternal life, which the Son of Man will give you. On him God the Father has placed his seal of approval.

Christ (John 6:27 NIV)

Abandon not the everlasting beauty for a beauty that must die, and set not your affections on this mortal world of dust.[9]

Bahá'u'lláh

If ye be seekers after this life and the vanities thereof, ye should have sought them while ye were still enclosed in your mothers' wombs, for at that time ye were continually approaching them, could ye but perceive it. Ye have, on the other hand, ever since ye were born and attained maturity, been all the while receding from the world and drawing closer to dust. Why, then, exhibit such greed in amassing the treasures of the earth, when your days are numbered and your chance is well-nigh lost? Will ye not, then, O heedless ones, shake off your slumber?[10]

Bahá'u'lláh

Seize the time, therefore, ere the glory of the divine springtime hath spent itself, and the Bird of Eternity ceased to warble its melody, that thy inner hearing may not be deprived of hearkening unto its call. This is My counsel unto thee and unto the beloved of God. Whosoever wisheth, let him turn thereunto; whosoever wisheth, let him turn away. God, verily, is independent of him and of that which he may see and witness.[11]

Bahá'u'lláh

Paradise is attainment of His good-pleasure and everlasting hell-fire His judgment through justice.[12]

The Báb

…no paradise is more glorious in the sight of God than attainment unto His good-pleasure.[13]

The Báb

Do not be afraid of those who kill the body but cannot kill the soul. Rather, be afraid of the One who can destroy both soul and body…   Christ (Matt. 10:28 NIV)

All that is with you passeth away, but that which is with God abideth. With a reward seemly for their best deeds will We surely recompense those who have patiently endured.   Qur'án 16:98

If anyone's name was not found written in the book of life, he was thrown into the lake of fire.   Christ (Rev. 20:15 NIV)

O people! Assuredly the promise of God is true. Let not the present life deceive you.   Qur'án 5:34

And set before them an analogy of the present life. It is as water which we send down from heaven, and the herb of the earth is mingled with it, and on the morrow it becometh dry stubble which the winds scatter...   Qur'án 18:43

Man—the true man—is soul, not body…[14]
'Abdu'l-Bahá

Soon will your swiftly-passing days be over, and the fame and riches, the comforts, the joys provided by this rubbish-heap, the world, will be gone without a trace.[15]   'Abdu'l-Bahá

Man is like a breath; his days are like a
fleeting shadow.   Psalms 144:4 NIV

Teach us to count how few days we have
and so gain wisdom of heart.
                         Psalms 90:12 NEB

The Greatness of Human Spirit

Thou art the day-star of the heavens of
My holiness, let not the defilement of the
world eclipse thy splendor.[16]   Bahá'u'lláh

Could ye apprehend with what wonders
of My munificence and bounty I have
willed to entrust your souls, ye would, of
a truth, rid yourselves of attachment to
all created things, and would gain a true
knowledge of your own selves—a knowledge which is the same as the comprehen-
sion of Mine own Being.[17]   Bahá'u'lláh

Heed not your weaknesses and frailty; fix
your gaze upon the invincible power of
the Lord, your God, the Almighty…Arise
in His name, put your trust wholly in Him,
and be assured of ultimate victory.[18]

                                   The Báb

No capacity is limited when led by the
Spirit of God![19]   'Abdu'l-Bahá

God's Purpose for Humankind

The purpose of the one true God in manifesting Himself...is to array every man with the mantle of a saintly character, and to adorn him with the ornament of holy and goodly deeds.[20]   Bahá'u'lláh

The purpose of God in creating man hath been, and will ever be, to enable him to know his Creator and to attain His Presence.[21]   Bahá'u'lláh

Through the Teachings of this Day Star of Truth every man will advance and develop until he attaineth the station at which he can manifest all the potential forces with which his inmost true self hath been endowed. It is for this very purpose that in every age and dispensation the Prophets of God and His chosen Ones have appeared amongst men...[22]

Bahá'u'lláh

He Who is the Day Spring of Truth is, no doubt, fully capable of rescuing from such remoteness wayward souls and of causing them to draw nigh unto His court and attain His Presence. "If God had pleased He had surely made all men one people." His purpose, however, is to enable the pure in spirit and the detached in heart to ascend, by virtue of their own innate powers, unto the shores of the Most Great Ocean, that thereby they who seek the Beauty of the All-Glorious may be distinguished and separated from the wayward and perverse. Thus hath it been ordained by the all-glorious and resplendent Pen.[23] Bahá'u'lláh

The purpose underlying Their revelation hath been to educate all men, that they may, at the hour of death, ascend, in the utmost purity and sanctity and with absolute detachment, to the throne of the Most High.[24]   Bahá'u'lláh

O Lord!...were it not for the sake of rendering service to Thee, my existence would avail me not.[25]   Bahá'u'lláh

Ye have, one and all, been called into being to seek His presence and to attain that exalted and glorious station.[26]   The Báb

Know thou that first and foremost in religion is the knowledge of God.[27]   The Báb

Love is the fundamental principle of God's purpose for man, and He has commanded us to love each other even as He loves us.[28]
                                    'Abdu'l-Bahá

The All-loving God created man to radiate the Divine light and to illumine the world by his words, action and life.[29]

'Abdu'l-Bahá

"What is the purpose of our lives?"…"To acquire virtues."[30] 'Abdu'l-Bahá

If no fruits of the Kingdom appear in the garden of his soul, man is not in the image and likeness of God, but if those fruits are forthcoming, he becomes the recipient of ideal bestowals and is enkindled with the fire of the love of God.[31] 'Abdu'l-Bahá

The highest development of man is his entrance into the divine Kingdom…[32]

'Abdu'l-Bahá

3

Prayers

Glory be to Thee, O Lord my God! Abase not him whom Thou hast exalted through the power of Thine everlasting sovereignty, and remove not far from Thee him whom Thou hast caused to enter the tabernacle of Thine eternity. Wilt Thou cast away, O my God, him whom Thou hast overshadowed with Thy Lordship, and wilt Thou turn away from Thee, O my Desire, him to whom Thou hast been a refuge? Canst Thou degrade him whom Thou hast uplifted, or forget him whom Thou didst enable to remember Thee?

Glorified, immensely glorified art Thou! Thou art He Who from everlasting hath been the King of the entire creation and its Prime Mover, and Thou wilt to everlasting remain the Lord of all created things and their Ordainer. Glorified art Thou, O my God! If Thou ceasest to be merciful unto Thy servants, who, then, will show mercy unto them; and if Thou refusest to succor Thy loved ones, who is there that can succor them?

Glorified, immeasurably glorified art Thou! Thou art adored in Thy truth, and Thee do we all, verily, worship; and Thou art manifest in Thy justice, and to Thee do we all, verily, bear witness. Thou art, in truth, beloved in Thy grace. No God is there but Thee, the Help in Peril, the Self-Subsisting.[1]   Bahá'u'lláh

Say: O God, my God! Thou hast committed into mine hands a trust from Thee, and hast now according to the good-pleasure of Thy Will called it back to Thyself. It is not for me, who am a handmaid of Thine, to say, whence is this to me or wherefore hath it happened, inasmuch as Thou art glorified in all Thine acts, and art to be obeyed in Thy decree. Thine handmaid, O my Lord, hath set her hopes on Thy grace and bounty. Grant that she may obtain that which will draw her nigh unto Thee, and will profit her in every world of Thine. Thou art the Forgiving, the All-Bountiful. There is none other God but Thee, the Ordainer, the Ancient of Days.[2]

Bahá'u'lláh

He is God, exalted is He, the Lord of loving-kindness and bounty!

Glory be unto Thee, Thou, O my God, the Lord Omnipotent. I testify to Thine omnipotence and Thy might, Thy sovereignty and Thy loving-kindness, Thy grace and Thy power, the oneness of Thy Being and the unity of Thine Essence, Thy sanctity and exaltation above the world of being and all that is therein.

O my God! Thou seest me detached from all save Thee, holding fast unto Thee and turning unto the ocean of Thy bounty, to the heaven of Thy favor, to the Daystar of Thy grace.

Lord! I bear witness that in Thy servant Thou hast reposed Thy Trust, and that is the Spirit wherewith Thou hast given life to the world.

I ask of Thee by the splendor of the Orb of Thy Revelation, mercifully to accept from him that which he hath achieved in Thy days. Grant then that he may be invested with the glory of Thy good-pleasure and adorned with Thine acceptance.

O my Lord! I myself and all created things bear witness unto Thy might, and I pray Thee not to turn away from Thyself this spirit that hath ascended unto Thee, unto Thy heavenly place, Thine exalted Paradise and Thy retreats of nearness, O Thou who art the Lord of all men!

Grant, then, O my God, that Thy servant may consort with Thy chosen ones, Thy saints and Thy Messengers in heavenly places that the pen cannot tell nor the tongue recount.

O My Lord, the poor one hath verily hastened unto the Kingdom of Thy wealth, the stranger unto his home within Thy precincts, he that is sore athirst to the heavenly river of Thy bounty. Deprive him not, O Lord, from his share of the banquet of Thy grace and from the favor of Thy bounty. Thou art in truth the Almighty, the Gracious, the All-Bountiful.

O my God, Thy Trust hath been returned unto Thee. It behooveth Thy grace and Thy bounty that have compassed Thy dominions on earth and in heaven, to vouchsafe unto Thy newly welcomed one Thy gifts and Thy bestowals, and the fruits of the tree of Thy grace! Powerful art Thou to do as Thou willest, there is none other God but Thee, the Gracious, the Most Bountiful, the Compassionate, the Bestower, the Pardoner, the Precious, the All-Knowing.

I testify, O my Lord, that Thou hast enjoined upon men to honor their guest, and he that hath ascended unto Thee hath verily reached Thee and attained Thy Presence. Deal with him then according to Thy grace and bounty! By Thy glory, I know of a certainty that Thou wilt not withhold Thyself from that which Thou hast commanded Thy servants, nor wilt Thou deprive him that hath clung to the cord of Thy bounty and hath ascended to the Dayspring of Thy wealth.

There is none other God but Thee, the One, the Single, the Powerful, the Omniscient, the Bountiful.[3]   Bahá'u'lláh

Lauded art Thou, O my God, my trespasses have waxed mighty and my sins have assumed grievous proportions. How disgraceful my plight will prove to be in Thy holy presence. I have failed to know Thee to the extent Thou didst reveal Thyself unto me; I have failed to worship Thee with a devotion worthy of Thy summons; I have failed to obey Thee through not treading the path of Thy love in the manner Thou didst inspire me.

Thy might beareth me witness, O my God, what befitteth Thee is far greater and more exalted than any being could attempt to accomplish. Indeed nothing can ever comprehend Thee as is worthy of Thee nor can any servile creature worship Thee as beseemeth Thine adoration. So perfect and comprehensive is Thy proof, O my God, that its inner essence transcendeth the description of any soul and so abundant are the outpourings of Thy gifts that no faculty can appraise their infinite range.

O my God! O my Master! I beseech Thee by Thy manifold bounties and by the pillars which sustain Thy throne of glory, to have pity on these lowly people who are powerless to bear the unpleasant things of this fleeting life, how much less then can they bear Thy chastisement in the life to come—a chastisement which is ordained by Thy justice, called forth by Thy wrath and will continue to exist for ever.

I beg Thee by Thyself, O my God, my Lord and my Master, to intercede in my behalf. I have fled from Thy justice unto Thy mercy. For my refuge I am seeking Thee and such as turn not away from Thy path, even for a twinkling of an eye—they for whose sake Thou didst create the creation as a token of Thy grace and bounty.[4]

The Báb

Praise be unto Thee, O Lord. Forgive us our sins, have mercy upon us and enable us to return unto Thee. Suffer us not to rely on aught else besides Thee, and vouchsafe unto us, through Thy bounty, that which Thou lovest and desirest and well beseemeth Thee. Exalt the station of them that have truly believed and forgive them with Thy gracious forgiveness. Verily Thou art the Help in Peril, the Self-Subsisting.[5]

The Báb

I beg Thy forgiveness, O my God, and implore pardon after the manner Thou wishest Thy servants to direct themselves to Thee. I beg of Thee to wash away our sins as befitteth Thy Lordship, and to forgive me, my parents, and those who in Thy estimation have entered the abode of Thy love in a manner which is worthy of Thy transcendent sovereignty and well beseemeth the glory of Thy celestial power.

O my God! Thou hast inspired my soul to offer its supplication to Thee, and but for Thee, I would not call upon Thee. Lauded and glorified art Thou; I yield Thee praise inasmuch as Thou didst reveal Thyself unto me, and I beg Thee to forgive me, since I have fallen short in my duty to know Thee and have failed to walk in the path of Thy love.[6]   The Báb

I am aware, O Lord, that my trespasses have covered my face with shame in Thy presence, and have burdened my back before Thee, have intervened between me and Thy beauteous countenance, have compassed me from every direction and

have hindered me on all sides from gaining access unto the revelations of Thy celestial power.

O Lord! If Thou forgivest me not, who is there then to grant pardon, and if Thou hast no mercy upon me who is capable of showing compassion? Glory be unto Thee, Thou didst create me when I was non-existent and Thou didst nourish me while I was devoid of any understanding. Praise be unto Thee, every evidence of bounty proceedeth from Thee and every token of grace emanateth from the treasuries of Thy decree.[7]   The Báb

O God our Lord! Protect us through Thy grace from whatsoever may be repugnant unto Thee and vouchsafe unto us that which well beseemeth Thee. Give us more out of Thy bounty and bless us. Pardon us for the things we have done and wash away our sins and forgive us with Thy gracious forgiveness. Verily Thou art the Most Exalted, the Self-Subsisting.

Thy loving providence hath encompassed all created things in the heavens and on the earth, and Thy forgiveness hath surpassed the whole creation. Thine is sovereignty;

in Thy hand are the Kingdoms of Creation and Revelation; in Thy right hand Thou holdest all created things and within Thy grasp are the assigned measures of forgiveness. Thou forgivest whomsoever among Thy servants Thou pleasest. Verily Thou art the Ever-Forgiving, the All-Loving. Nothing whatsoever escapeth Thy knowledge, and naught is there which is hidden from Thee.

O God our Lord! Protect us through the potency of Thy might, enable us to enter Thy wondrous surging ocean, and grant us that which well befitteth Thee.

Thou art the Sovereign Ruler, the Mighty Doer, the Exalted, the All-loving.[8]

The Báb

Glory be unto Thee, O God. How can I make mention of Thee while Thou art sanctified from the praise of all mankind. Magnified be Thy Name, O God, Thou art the King, the Eternal Truth; Thou knowest what is in the heavens and on the earth, and unto Thee must all return. Thou hast sent down Thy divinely-ordained Revelation according to a clear measure. Praised art Thou, O Lord! At Thy behest Thou dost render victorious whomsoever Thou willest, through the hosts of heaven and earth and whatsoever existeth between them. Thou art the Sovereign, the Eternal Truth, the Lord of invincible might.

Glorified art Thou, O Lord, Thou forgivest at all times the sins of such among Thy servants as implore Thy pardon. Wash away my sins and the sins of those who seek Thy forgiveness at dawn, who pray to Thee in the day-time and in the night season, who yearn after naught save God, who offer up whatsoever God hath graciously bestowed upon them, who celebrate Thy praise at morn and eventide, and who are not remiss in their duties.[9]

The Báb

O my God! O Thou forgiver of sins, bestower of gifts, dispeller of afflictions!

Verily, I beseech Thee to forgive the sins of such as have abandoned the physical garment and have ascended to the spiritual world.

O my Lord! Purify them from trespasses, dispel their sorrows, and change their darkness into light. Cause them to enter the garden of happiness, cleanse them with the most pure water, and grant them

105

to behold Thy splendors on the loftiest mount.[10]

'Abdu'l-Bahá

O my God! O my God! Verily Thy servant, humble before the majesty of Thy divine supremacy, lowly at the door of Thy oneness, hath believed in Thee and in Thy verses, hath testified to Thy word, hath been enkindled with the fire of Thy love, hath been immersed in the depths of the ocean of Thy knowledge, hath been attracted by Thy breezes, hath relied upon Thee, hath turned his face to Thee, hath offered his supplications to Thee, and hath been assured of Thy pardon and forgiveness. He hath abandoned this mortal life and hath flown to the kingdom of immortality, yearning for the favor of meeting Thee.

O Lord, glorify his station, shelter him under the pavilion of Thy supreme mercy, cause him to enter Thy glorious paradise, and perpetuate his existence in Thine exalted rose garden, that he may plunge into the sea of light in the world of mysteries.

Verily, Thou art the Generous, the Powerful, the Forgiver and the Bestower.[11]

'Abdu'l-Bahá

A Special Prayer Recited at the Time of Burial

(The Prayer for the Dead is the only Bahá'í obligatory prayer that is to be recited in congregation; it is to be recited by one believer while all present stand in silence. Bahá'u'lláh has clarified that this prayer is required only when the deceased is over the age of fifteen, that its recital must precede internment, and that there is no requirement to face the Qiblih [the Shrine of Bahá'u'lláh] during its recitation.)[12]

On the finger of the departed should be placed a ring on which this prayer is inscribed: "I came forth from God, and return unto Him, detached from all save Him, holding fast to His Name, the Merciful, the Compassionate."[13]

O my God! This is Thy servant and the son of Thy servant who hath believed in Thee and in Thy signs, and set his face towards Thee, wholly detached from all except Thee. Thou art, verily, of those who show mercy the most merciful.

Deal with him, O Thou Who forgivest the sins of men and concealest their faults, as beseemeth the heaven of Thy bounty and the ocean of Thy grace. Grant him admission within the precincts of Thy transcendent mercy that was before the foundation of earth and heaven. There is no God but Thee, the Ever-Forgiving, the Most Generous.

("Alláh'u'Abhá" is said once; then the first of the six verses is recited nineteen times. Then "Alláh'u'Abhá" is said again, followed by the second verse, which is recited nineteen times, and so on.)

We all, verily, worship God.

We all, verily, bow down before God.

We all, verily, are devoted unto God.

We all, verily, give praise unto God.

We all, verily, yield thanks unto God.

We all, verily, are patient in God.

(If the dead be a woman, let him say: This is Thy handmaiden and the daughter of Thy handmaiden, etc...)[14]   Bahá'u'lláh

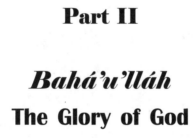

Part II

Bahá'u'lláh
The Glory of God

Bahá'u'lláh
The Glory of God

As stated in the introduction, a purpose of "Blazon-His-Name" series is to introduce *Bahá'u'lláh—the Glory of God*—to the western world. He is the One promised in all Scriptures. He has come to establish the heavenly Kingdom both within our soul and without. Only once in a thousand years a spiritual Figure, a Messenger and Redeemer from God, such as Bahá'u'lláh appears upon the earth. You now have a chance to know Him, to get a glimpse of His glory—a glory that will in time fill the earth:

> For the earth will be filled with the knowledge of *the glory of the Lord*, as the waters cover the sea.
>
> Habakkuk 2:14 NIV

> …all the earth shall be filled with *the glory of the Lord*.
> Numbers 14:21

Who Was Bahá'u'lláh?

In examining the evidence for the One who has claimed to speak the Word of God, the most vital questions are these: Who was He? What was He like? How did He live? What happened to Him? Here are a few features of Bahá'u'lláh's life, adapted mostly from a book entitled *Some Answered Questions*:

Bahá'u'lláh was born in 1817, in Persia, to a rich and noble family. He died in 1892, as a prisoner and exile in the Holy Land. As an infant, He astonished His parents by His uniqueness and distinctions. His father related that He would never cry or scream. "You don't know," he said, "what a potential He has, how intelligent He is! He is like a flame of fire, and in His tender years superior to young people."[1] Bahá'u'lláh's father was so captivated by Him that he wrote a piece of poetry in his son's honor, inscribed it on a plaque, and hung it on the wall of a summer mansion in which Bahá'u'lláh lived. The

content of the poetry shows that the father sensed
the divine destiny of his Son:

> When thou enterest the sacred abode of the Be-
> loved say:
> "I am at thy command.
> This is the home of love; enter with reverence.
> This is holy ground; remove thy shoes when
> thou enterest here."[2]

People were attracted by Bahá'u'lláh's many distinctions. He did not attend any school, yet astonished
people by His wisdom and knowledge. Even His
enemies testified to His greatness. Great thinkers
flocked to His presence, asking Him their most dif-
ficult questions. They said, "This man is unique in
all perfections."

> He had an extraordinary power of attraction,
> which was felt by all. People always crowded
> around Him. Ministers and people of the Court
> would surround Him, and the children also were
> devoted to Him. When He was only thirteen or
> fourteen years old He became renowned for His
> learning. He would converse on any subject and
> solve any problem presented to Him. In large
> gatherings He would...explain intricate religious
> questions. All of them used to listen to Him with
> the greatest interest.[3]

He showed no interest in politics:

> When Bahá'u'lláh was twenty two years old,
> His father died, and the Government wished

Him to succeed to His father's position in the Ministry...but Bahá'u'lláh did not accept the offer. Then the Prime Minister said: "Leave him to himself. Such a position is unworthy of him. He has some higher aim in view. I cannot understand him, but I am convinced that he is destined for some lofty career. His thoughts are not like ours. Let him alone."[4]

Bahá'u'lláh was known especially for His generosity and love for the poor:

He was most generous, giving abundantly to the poor. None who came to Him were turned away. The doors of His house were open to all.[5]

One day Bahá'u'lláh sent 'Abdu'l-Bahá, His eldest Son, to inspect the work of the shepherds who were taking care of His sheep. 'Abdu'l-Bahá was a small child at the time, and the persecutions against Bahá'u'lláh and His family had not yet started. Bahá'u'lláh then had a good deal of land in the mountains and owned large herds of sheep. When the inspection was finished and 'Abdu'l-Bahá was ready to leave, the man who had accompanied Him said, "It is your father's custom to leave a gift for each shepherd." 'Abdu'l-Bahá became silent for a while, because He did not have anything to give them. The man, however, insisted that the shepherds were expecting something. Then 'Abdu'l-Bahá had an idea that made Him very happy! He would give the shepherds the sheep they were taking care of! Bahá'u'lláh was very much pleased when He heard about

'Abdu'l-Bahá's generous thoughts towards the shepherds. He humorously remarked that everyone had better take good care of 'Abdu'l-Bahá because someday He would give Himself away. Of course, this is exactly what 'Abdu'l-Bahá did for the rest of His life. He gave everything He had, each and every moment of His life, to humanity, to unite us and bring us true happiness.[6]

Bahá'u'lláh was also known for His courage to stand against the powerful who would abuse their power:

All classes of men marveled at His miraculous success in emerging unscathed from the most perilous encounters. Nothing short of Divine protection, they thought, could have ensured His safety on such occasions...In His constant association, during those days, with the highest dignitaries of the realm...He was never content simply to accede to the views they expressed or the claims they advanced. He would, at their gatherings, fearlessly champion the cause of truth, would assert the rights of the downtrodden, defending the weak and protecting the innocent.[7]

Bahá'u'lláh spent the early part of His life in the utmost joy and happiness. But He later became a target of prejudice and persecution. Thousands of fanatical believers rose against Him. Religious leaders were terrified of losing their power. They said, "This man intends to destroy religion, law, the nation, and the empire." (People made the same accusations against Jesus.) He faced His enemies with the utmost courage, showing no weakness or fear.

Bahá'u'lláh endured nearly 40 years of imprisonment and exile, yet He never complained. No human being can imagine the extent of His sufferings. Among His sufferings was imprisonment in an infamous dungeon in Tihrán, known as the Black Pit or Black Dungeon, where He was kept for four months. In that dungeon He endured every conceivable pain and anguish:

- *Total darkness*: The underground prison had neither lights nor windows.

- *A terrible stench*: About 150 of the worst criminals were thrown in that dark, deep, and damp dungeon with no air circulation or sanitary facilities. The ground was covered with several inches of filthy mud and mire.

- *Hunger and thirst*: For the first three days and nights Bahá'u'lláh received neither food nor water.

- *Severe pain and lack of mobility*: Bahá'u'lláh's feet were put in stocks, and on His neck was placed a chain so heavy that He was unable to hold Himself upright. To hold the weight of the chain, Bahá'u'lláh had to press His hands against the ground covered with slime up to His wrists. From the weight of the harsh metal, His neck became inflamed and injured.

- *Little if any sleep*: Bahá'u'lláh could hardly sleep under those horrible conditions.

- *Lack of clothes*: His outer garments were stripped away on His way to the prison.

- *Illness*: Because of the unsanitary conditions, Bahá'u'lláh suffered grave illness.

- *Being poisoned*: He also suffered pain from consuming poison placed in His food.

- *Homelessness*: All His properties were confiscated.

- *Loneliness*: "During this time none of His friends were able to get access to Him."[8]

- *Being surrounded by the worst criminals* who had little if any hope of survival or freedom.

- *Anxiety about His family*: Bahá'u'lláh's family members, including His young children, were left at the mercy of fanatical mobs, filled with rage and incited to seek revenge. (His Son, 'Abdu'l-Bahá, was then 9 years old.)

- *Deep grief and concern for His devoted and distinguished disciples*, who were being hunted down, tortured, and killed by enraged mobs outside the prison.

- *Concern about the future*: From that prison Bahá'u'lláh was banished to strange lands. As foretold in a prophecy (Matt. 25:41-46), He became a stranger (an exile). Never again did He see His homeland.

- *Deep sorrow* for those who were rejecting God's choicest blessings and bounties.*

---

* The Bible contains numerous prophecies that predict suffering for Jesus in His Second Advent. For a review of such prophecies, see *King of Kings*.

It was in this dungeon that Bahá'u'lláh expressed the first intimations of His Divine Mission:

> One night, in a dream, these exalted words were heard on every side: "Verily, We shall render Thee victorious by Thyself and by Thy Pen. Grieve Thou not for that which hath befallen Thee, neither be Thou afraid, for Thou art in safety. Erelong will God raise up the treasures of the earth—men who will aid Thee through Thyself and through Thy Name..."[9]

Bahá'u'lláh repeatedly stated that He spoke only by God's command, and not of His own choosing. He declared:

> Think ye, O people, that I hold within My grasp the control of God's ultimate Will and Purpose? ...Had the ultimate destiny of God's Faith been in Mine hands, I would have never consented, even though for one moment, to manifest Myself unto you, nor would I have allowed one word to fall from My lips. Of this God Himself is, verily, a witness.[10]

> This is but a leaf which the winds of the will of thy Lord, the Almighty, the All-Praised, have stirred. Can it be still when the tempestuous winds are blowing? Nay, by Him Who is the Lord of all Names and Attributes![11]

Bahá'u'lláh's arrest and imprisonment in that dungeon give us only a glimpse of the sufferings He endured for nearly 40 years in three different countries. How could anyone survive the scourge of such unrelenting pressures? How much pain can a human being endure? Why would God allow the One He loved the most to go through so much suffering? Did not Jesus endure similar ordeals?

> Worldly friends, seeking their own good, appear to love one the other, whereas the true Friend [Bahá'u'lláh] hath loved and doth love you for your own sakes; indeed He hath suffered for your guidance countless afflictions. Be not disloyal to such a Friend, nay rather hasten unto Him.[12]
>   Bahá'u'lláh

The religious leaders feared Bahá'u'lláh's influence, so they had Him exiled to another land. They thought in a strange land His influence would die out. But the result was that His charm captivated many more disciples. They exiled Him again and again. The results were the same—a spreading of His influence. Finally, they sent Him to the worst place they could find: a prison for murderers and thieves, located in a remote city ('Akká) with a dreadful climate and foul water. The sufferings Bahá'u'lláh endured in 'Akká surpassed even those He experienced in the Black Dungeon.

> Bahá'u'lláh was placed in a barren, filthy room, while His followers were crowded into another, the floor of which was covered with mud. Ten soldiers were posted to stand guard over them. To add further to their misery, the exiles, parched from a long day in the hot sun, soon found that the only water available to them was unfit for consumption. Mothers were unable to feed their babies, and infants cried for hours...

Under these conditions, all but 'Abdu'l-Bahá [Bahá'u'lláh's Son] and one other, fell ill. Within a matter of days three men died. The officials denied the prisoners permission to leave the citadel to bury them, and the guards demanded payment before removing the bodies. Bahá'u'lláh ordered that His prayer rug, the only item of any value that He possessed, be sold to cover the cost of the burial. The guards pocketed the money and buried the men in the clothes in which they died...

Three days after the exiles' arrival, the Sultán's edict was read aloud in the mosque. It sentenced Bahá'u'lláh, His family, and His companions to life imprisonment and expressly forbade the exiles to associate with one another or with local inhabitants.[13]

During Bahá'u'lláh's imprisonment in 'Akká, His young son was pacing the roof of the prison, "wrapped in devotions, when he fell through a skylight. Mortally wounded, his dying wish to his Father was that his life might be a ransom for those who were prevented from attaining Bahá'u'lláh's presence."[14] In a prayer, Bahá'u'lláh speaks of the sacrifice of His son:

I have, O my Lord, offered up that which Thou hast given Me, that Thy servants may be quickened, and all that dwell on earth be united.[15]

Here Bahá'u'lláh explains why He accepted so much pain and suffering:

> The Ancient Beauty [Bahá'u'lláh] hath consented to be bound with chains that mankind may be released from its bondage, and hath accepted to be made a prisoner...that the whole world may attain unto true liberty. He hath drained to its dregs the cup of sorrow, that all the peoples of the earth may attain unto abiding joy, and be filled with gladness. This is of the mercy of your Lord, the Compassionate, the Most Merciful. We have accepted to be abased...that ye may be exalted, and have suffered manifold afflictions, that ye might prosper and flourish. He Who hath come to build anew the whole world, behold, how they...have forced Him to dwell within the most desolate of cities![16]

Despite this severe repression, Bahá'u'lláh's influence continued to spread, His glory became more evident. From behind prison walls, He triumphed over all His enemies.

> For if this idea...is of human origin, it will collapse; but if it is from God, you will never be able to put them [the believers] down, and you risk finding yourself at war with God.
>
> Acts 5:38-39

When Bahá'u'lláh was exiled to the Holy Land, those aware of biblical prophecies suddenly realized what had happened: Bahá'u'lláh's enemies had, unknowingly, become the very instruments for the fulfillment of prophecies about Him because the Bible predicts repeatedly that the Redeemer of the Last Days will come to the Holy Land. Those who had wished to destroy Him became the means of His triumph. (For a review of these prophecies and many others, see *I Shall Come Again, Lord of Lords,* and *King of Kings.*)

In 1868, while under arrest, Bahá'u'lláh addressed the kings and rulers of the earth, asking them to act with justice and to work for peace. With the exception of Queen Victoria, they ignored His call. He predicted their downfall and His own triumph.

Among these sovereigns was Napoleon III. Bahá'u'lláh asked him to investigate the reason for His imprisonment. The sovereign did not respond. Bahá'u'lláh sent a second letter, predicting his downfall. Soon thereafter, in 1870, war between Germany and France broke out. Everything seemed to be in Napoleon's favor, yet he was defeated, dishonored, and debased. According to *The Fall of Paris*:

> History knows of perhaps no more startling instance of what the Greeks called peripateia, the terrible fall from prideful heights. Certainly no nation in modern times, so replete with apparent grandeur and opulent in material achievement, has ever been subjected to a worse humiliation in so short a time.[17]

Other sovereigns addressed by Bahá'u'lláh encountered similar fates. Every prediction that Bahá'u'lláh made was fulfilled. These are discussed in a book titled *The Prisoner and the King*, by William Sears.

Bahá'u'lláh's greatness touched even those who did not follow Him. They wrote about His knowledge,

His kindness, and His patience. They flocked to His presence and marveled at His wondrous works.

How often would one of His bitter enemies say to himself, "When I see Him, I will argue with Him and defeat Him in this way..." But when faced with Bahá'u'lláh, he would find himself speechless—unable to utter a word.

Bahá'u'lláh declared His willingness to be tested. To leave the religious leaders with no excuse, Bahá'u'lláh said that He was willing to perform any miracle that they requested. The only condition He set was that, after the miracle was performed, they would acknowledge the validity of His claim. The religious leaders declined to accept the condition. (God has always refused requests to perform miracles to prove His power, see Matt. 4:7. We cannot be sure why Bahá'u'lláh accepted this request. Perhaps one reason was that He knew it would be rejected.)

Bahá'u'lláh demonstrated His dependence on the divine and detachment from worldly desires by associating with the poor and the humble and avoiding the powerful and the pompous.[18] A famous figure wanted to meet Bahá'u'lláh. But to be seen with Bahá'u'lláh meant danger. He sent a message asking to meet with Him secretly. In response, Bahá'u'lláh sent him a piece of poetry to this effect: "Unless you have a desire to sacrifice your life, don't come here. This is the way if you wish to meet Bahá. If you are unprepared for this journey, don't come, and don't bring trouble." The man dared not take the risk of endangering his life and declined.

For nearly 50 years Bahá'u'lláh faced bitter enemies who killed thousands of His followers yet failed to destroy Him. Repeatedly they planned and plotted against Him, but to no avail.

Are these marks of distinction not similar to those found in the life of Jesus?

> We must be just and acknowledge what an Educator this Glorious Being was, what marvelous signs were manifested by Him, and what power and might have been realized in the world through Him.[19]   'Abdu'l-Bahá

> My deeds done in my Father's name are my credentials.   Christ (John 10:25)

> Accept the evidence of my deeds.
>   Christ (John 10:38)

Part III

Books that Can Change Your Destiny

- *Bahá'í Scriptures Available in English*

- *Books on the Bahá'í Faith by the Same Author*

Bahá'í Scriptures
Available in English

Bahá'u'lláh's Works

Seek ye out the book of Jehovah and read...
Isaiah 34:16

Gleanings from the
Writings of Bahá'u'lláh

The most complete and comprehensive reference on Bahá'u'lláh's Works available in English. This book, which is a compilation from the Writings of Bahá'u'lláh, covers a wide spectrum of precepts ranging from the purpose of man's creation, his duty and destiny, to the manifold mysteries of divine Wisdom.

Prayers and Meditations
By Bahá'u'lláh

Bahá'u'lláh has left a rich repository of prayers pertaining to every human hope and aspiration, dream or desire. Thus, in this dispensation, the seekers of serenity, guidance, and inspiration can select and recite prayers and meditations revealed and blessed by the Pen of the Redeemer of the age, the revealer of divine Purpose.

Bahá'u'lláh has also written many prayers express-
ing His own supplication and servitude before God.
Such prayers offer an intimate knowledge of
Bahá'u'lláh's own self—His indomitable spirit, His
unswerving love for the Creator and for humanity,
His steadfastness in His claim, His determination
before the onrush of adversities, His absolute trust
in God, and His loving counsel to all those athirst
for truth.

The Hidden Words
of Bahá'u'lláh

No other of Bahá'u'lláh's works so succinctly offers
the reader as complete and as representative a
sample of the ethical fruits of the new Revelation
as *The Hidden Words*. It is a small book filled with
gems, a treasure-house of celestial Wisdom, a divine guide to the unfoldment and ennoblement of
the human spirit.

All the requirements for attaining purity and self-
fulfillment are stated in the most exquisite and lofty
language. Everything that the soul must seek or
surrender, everything that a spiritual seeker must
know or must do to direct the course of his or her
spiritual destiny is concisely and clearly revealed
and set forth by the pen of the Supreme Messenger—the Revealer of hidden wisdom and divine
mysteries.

The Seven Valleys and the Four Valleys

Perhaps the most mystical of Bahá'u'lláh's works available in English. It unfolds and enumerates the stages of seeker's journey towards God; revealing, in a language at once poetic and perplexing, his potential for attaining perfection and nobility, and his sublime and celestial destiny, if he but turns to the light instead of darkness, seeks the gems of divine wisdom instead of the perishable joys of flesh, and undertakes to tread the long but wondrous and enchanting path of purification and illumination.

Epistle to the Son of the Wolf

Addressed to a cruel and cunning Muslim clergyman who, along with his father, inflicted death, distress, and torment on some of Bahá'u'lláh's most beloved and most distinguished disciples. Though addressed to a symbol of denial, it is a call to humanity as a whole. This weighty volume covers and clarifies many illuminating and inspiring arrays of precepts.

The Summons of the Lord of Hosts

Contains some of Bahá'u'lláh's Epistles or Tablets addressed to the kings and rulers of the world, to its religious leaders, and to humanity in general. These Tablets comprise Bahá'u'lláh's most emphatic words on His claim and on His station as the supreme Savior of humankind, the King of Kings, the Glory of the Lord, the Desire of the Nations, the Everlasting Father, the Prince of Peace, the Lord of the Vineyard, Christ returned in the Glory of the Father, the Inaugurator of the Cycle of Fulfillment, and the Promised One of all ages and religions.

The Book of Certitude✣

This book responds to questions raised by a seeker of truth. It unseals "the sealed Wine of mysteries," and unveils the symbolism and the essence of all the scriptures of the past, indicates how the seeker of truth can rise above the prevailing perplexity and confusion, how he or she can move from doubt to certitude, and from unbelief to belief.

It offers proofs of divine Revelation, portrays in a moving language man's refusal to accept and acknowledge, in every age, the gift of divine Guidance, and conveys in a unique tone and style the dramatic story of the unfoldment of the perennial Faith of God, the unveiling of the eternal Truth.

✣Also known as *The Kitáb-i-Íqán.*

Other Bahá'í Writings
Available in English

By Bahá'u'lláh:

The Most Holy Book
Tablets of Bahá'u'lláh
Gems of Divine Mysteries
Tabernacle of Unity

═══════════════

By the Báb:

Selections from the Writings of the Báb

═══════════════

By 'Abdu'l-Bahá:

Some Answered Questions
Foundations of World Unity
The Secret of Divine Civilization
Paris Talks
Selections from the Writings of 'Abdu'l-Bahá
The Promulgation of Universal Peace
A Traveller's Narrative

Books on the Bahá'í Faith by the Same Author

- *Evidence for the Bahá'í Faith*
- *History and Teachings*
- *The Afterlife*
- *Forthcoming Books*

Evidence for the Bahá'í Faith

I Shall Come Again
522 Pages
Volume I

*That is the day when I come like a thief.
Happy the man who stays awake.*
Christ (Rev. 16:15)

*Do not let Him find you sleeping. What I
say to you, I say to everyone: "Watch!"*
Christ (Mark 13:36)

Did you know that the Bible contains 16 time prophecies concerning the year of the Second Advent? No wonder so many scholars discovered the same date. Did you also know that all those 16 prophecies point to the same year: 1844? *Bahá'ís believe that the promise of the Second Advent has already been fulfilled, precisely as predicted.* Christ did return in 1844, "*like a thief*," in a way that *the News of His coming did not draw much attention*. And as the Book of Revelation predicts, God gave Him a new name: *Bahá'u'lláh*, meaning *the Glory of God*.

Obviously *we expect you to be very skeptical*, but we invite you *to stay spiritually awake, to "watch," to pay close attention, and to investigate this most glorious News*. How can you do this? Start your search by examining the evidence presented in *I Shall Come Again*, the first of a six-volume series on the fulfillment of biblical prophecies by *Bahá'u'lláh, the Glory of God*.

I Shall Come Again, written after three decades of research, takes you step by step through 16 prophecies that point to 1844, and hundreds of other prophecies, concerning the return of Christ. It proves how these prophecies, without exception, were fulfilled by *Bahá'u'lláh (the Glory of God)* and His martyred Herald, *the Báb (the Gate)*, who appeared in 1844. *I Shall Come Again* is one of the most fascinating books of our time. If you have faith in God's promises and a desire to know the truth, you will receive incomparable joy and hope from reading it.

History shows that no false prophet has ever been able to prove his claim by the evidence of fulfilled prophecies. Christian scholars often regard Hebrew prophecies as the most conclusive and convincing evidence of Jesus' divine Mission.

Let us consider a statement from Dr. Norman Geisler, president of Southern Evangelical Seminary, "who has published countless articles in academic journals and has authored over fifty books, including *Baker Encyclopedia of Christian Apologetics*." Dr. Geisler makes the following statement concerning the prophecies that point to the First Advent of Jesus:

Some have suggested...that the prophecies were accidentally fulfilled in Jesus. In other words, he happened to be in the right place at the right time...If there is a God who is in control of the universe, as we have said, then chance is ruled out. Furthermore, it is unlikely that these events would have converged in the life of one man. Mathematicians have calculated the probability of 16 predictions being fulfilled in one man at 1 in 10^{45}...

But it is not just a logical improbability that rules out this theory [of chance]; it is the moral implausibility of an all-powerful and all-knowing God letting things get out of control so that all his plans for prophetic fulfillment are ruined by someone who just happened to be in the right place at the right time. God cannot lie, nor can he break a promise (Heb. 6:18). So we must conclude that he did not allow his prophetic promises to be thwarted by chance. All the evidence points to Jesus as the divinely appointed fulfillment of the Messianic prophecies. He was God's man confirmed by God's signs. In brief, if God made the predictions to be fulfilled in the life of Christ, then he would not allow them to be fulfilled in the life of any other. The God of truth would not allow a lie to be confirmed as true.

Imagine if the News of the Return of Jesus is true and you choose not to investigate and not to know Him! Imagine also if the News of His Return is true and your investigation leads you to recognize Him!

I shall come again and receive you to myself, so that where I am you may be also.

Christ (John 14:3)

"He, verily, is come with His Kingdom, and all the atoms cry aloud: 'Lo! The Lord is come in His great majesty!'" "Behold how He hath come down from the heaven of His grace, girded with power and invested with sovereignty. Is there any doubt concerning His signs?"

Bahá'u'lláh (the Glory of God)

Lord of Lords

634 Pages

Volume II

This volume presents hundreds of biblical prophecies concerning the Central Figures of the Bahá'í Faith—the Báb, Bahá'u'lláh, 'Abdu'l-Bahá—as well as Shoghi Effendi (the Guardian of the Bahá'í

Faith), the Universal House of Justice (the supreme administrative body in the Bahá'í Faith), the Bahá'ís (the followers of Bahá'u'lláh), the Bahá'í teachings, and the Book of Bahá'í Laws (*The Kitáb-i-Aqdas*).

Lord of Lords presents six fulfillments for Daniel's prophecy of 1335, and shows their connection to the Bahá'í Faith. The book also presents *86 similarities between Jesus and the Báb*, who is called *"One like a Son of Man."*

Christian scholars often apply the statistical laws to the prophecies of Hebrew Scriptures to prove the divine station of Jesus. *Lord of Lords* applies the same laws to the prophecies of both Hebrew and Christian Scriptures to prove the divine station of the Báb and Bahá'u'lláh.

Lord of Lords shows that the probability of biblical prophecies coming true in the Bahá'í Faith by chance alone is about 1 in 10^{80}. The number 10^{80} is equal to the number of atoms in the known universe! What does this evidence indicate? *It indicates that if anyone could pick a specific atom in the universe by chance, he could then claim that the biblical prophecies fulfilled in the Bahá'í Faith also happened by chance!* The proof presented in this volume is so compelling it can convince even the most skeptic seeker!

...the desire of all nations shall come...
Haggai 2:7

He who is the Desired One is come in His transcendent majesty...Better is this for you than all ye possess. *Bahá'u'lláh (the Glory of God)*

For the Son of man shall come in the glory of his Father...   *Christ (Matt. 16:27)*

I have come in the shadows of the clouds of glory, and am invested by God with invincible sovereignty.   *Bahá'u'lláh (the Glory of God)*

King of Kings
510 Pages
Volume III

This is the third of the six-volume series. This volume also presents hundreds of biblical prophecies concerning the advent of the Bahá'í Faith. Four of its chapters show that, contrary to what most people —both Christians and Jews—believe, *the Bible predicts suffering and severe persecution for the Redeemer of our time. King of Kings* also presents many prophecies, in the course of two chapters, to show that according to both Testaments, the title of the Redeemer of our age (known to Christians as the Second Coming of Christ and to the Jews as the Messiah) is "*the Glory of God*," the English translation of the original title "*Bahá'u'lláh*."

A chapter discusses the many reasons why people deny and persecute their promised Messenger and Redeemer in every age, and then later claim that if they had lived at the time of His Advent they would not be among the deniers!

Many Christians expect the coming of the Antichrist. *King of Kings* presents two chapters to show the fulfillment of this expectation by two deceptive figures who opposed *Bahá'u'lláh, the Glory of God*, with all their might, and tried in vain to destroy Him and establish themselves as the Central Figures of the Bahá'í Faith.

I Shall Come Again, *Lord of Lords*, and *King of Kings* prove that once again God has spoken to humanity, that He has fulfilled His promises, and has manifested His great glory and power by sending two supreme Messengers and Redeemers— *Bahá'u'lláh, and His martyred Herald, the Báb*—to guide our bewildered world to unity, peace, and justice, and to lead our wandering souls to His heavenly Mansions. Not investigating this Message of hope and fulfillment is to deprive yourself of the very source of all wisdom and the very purpose of coming to this world.

> *I have come down from heaven...*
>
> *Christ (John 6:38)*

> *Say, God is my witness! The Promised One Himself [Bahá'u'lláh] hath come down from heaven...with the hosts of revelation on His right, and the angels of inspiration on His left...* *Bahá'u'lláh (the Glory of God)*

> *Behold, I come like a thief! Blessed is he who stays awake...* *Christ (Rev. 16:15)*

> *Blessed the slumberer who is awakened... Blessed the ear that hath heard, and the eye*

that hath seen, and the heart that hath turned unto Him...   *Bahá'u'lláh (the Glory of God)*

What do others say about:

I Shall Come Again, Lord of Lords, King of Kings?

A scholarly work of meticulous research. Appealing to reason and applying the scientific method to prophetic scripture, it demonstrates that God has once again revealed Himself to humankind and has provided hope for unity and peace on this planet.   **John Paul Vader, M.D.**
Author of: *For the Good of Mankind*

A book with a message of hope and fulfillment, a message that can transform our planet into a place of peace, into a kingdom that has been the dream and hope of humanity since the dawn of history...a scholarly, comprehensive, and fascinating work that has been long overdue. No wonder it took over three decades to complete it.   **Hon. Dorothy W. Nelson**
Judge, U. S. Court of Appeals, 9th Circuit

A story with an incredible ending that is made credible by the sheer weight of evidence. It is a must for anyone interested in the proofs of the advent of the Promised One of all ages.

John Huddleston
Former Chief of Budget and Planning Division, International Monetary Fund, Author of *The Earth Is But One Country*

...a treasure house of great value for both Bahá'ís and seekers. **Adib Taherzadeh**
Author and Scholar

I am in awe at the extent of research you have undertaken! **Waldo Boyd**
Writer and Editor

Your work never fails to astound me. The effort and breadth of your knowledge both of the Bible and other literature as well as the depth of your understanding of Bahá'í Scripture is truly amazing. Also, a hallmark of your work is your thoroughness. Anyone who believes in biblical prophecy, and reads these volumes with an open mind, cannot fail to be convinced.

Dr. Tom Rowe
Professor of Psychology

Your work is the best I've seen on biblical prophecies and proofs of Bahá'u'lláh's Revelation. You offer so much information in relatively few pages. Your many references prove clearly the book's central claim. Your language is simple and exciting. You take the reader through a complete spiritual and prophetic adventure. Your approach is modest, yet dynamic. I pray it will excite all your readers as it has excited me. **Joe Killeen**
Bible Scholar, Former Minister

There are few works by a single author that can rival Dr. Motlagh's in their sheer scope, depth and thoroughness of scholarship. Without doubt, future Bahá'ís will thank Dr. Motlagh for his achievements, that are, in my opinion, not only astonishing—they are heroic.

An important work that will be referenced by future Bahá'í scholars for millennia to come.

Robert F. Riggs
Aerospace and Marine Scientist, Inventor,
Author of *The Apocalypse Unsealed*

By writing these volumes Dr. Motlagh has made a momentous contribution to our understanding of biblical prophecy. As a former Baptist minister, I urge all Christians to investigate the news of the return of our Lord as presented in **I Shall Come Again, Lord of Lords,** *and* **King of Kings.** *"Arise, shine, for your light has come, and the glory of the Lord rises upon you" (Isa. 60:1).*

Mel Campbell
Former Baptist Minister

Come Now, Let Us Reason Together
286 Pages

This book is written in response to the objections raised by a pastor against the Bahá'í Faith. It removes all the main obstacles that prevent Christians from recognizing the return of the Son in the glory of the Father, from acknowledging the promised

Redeemer of our time—***Bahá'u'lláh, the Glory of God***. Once you start reading this book, you will find it hard to put down.

The Glory of The Father
329 pages

One way to prove that Bahá'u'lláh fulfills the promise of the Second Advent is to compare Him with Jesus Christ. ***The Glory of the Father: The Case for Christ and Bahá'u'lláh***, does exactly that. It compares Jesus and Bahá'u'lláh in 35 different ways. A fair-minded, even a skeptical, reader cannot escape this conclusion: If Jesus is the One He claims to be, so must be Bahá'u'lláh. A sincere Christian cannot in good faith accept One and reject the other. It will be like having twin children, but loving only one of them!

In addition, ***The Glory of the Father*** offers a summary of some of the most significant prophecies presented in ***I Shall Come Again***, ***Lord of Lords***, and ***King of Kings***.

History and Teachings

***On Wings of
Destiny***

274 Pages

On Wings of Destiny is based on a dialogue between two friends. Reading it is like joining a circle of friends and participating in a "fireside chat."

The prime purpose of the book is to inspire you—and anyone else who values his soul and spiritual life—to recognize that ***in this world you have an awesome responsibility: you must choose your everlasting destiny. That choice has unimaginable consequences that will endure beyond death for all eternity***. Failing to make a choice is also a choice. This book invites you to make every effort to discover God's plan for you and to follow that plan.

On Wings of Destiny shows that the only way you can attain true joy and happiness in all the worlds of God is to cultivate your spiritual potential and to draw nearer and nearer to God. If you value your soul and wish to choose your destiny in the light of knowledge and freedom, take the time to listen to this inspiring "fireside chat" to discover how the Bahá'í teachings can help you attain contentment, fulfill your life's purpose, and discover your divine destiny: Heaven's most glorious gift to you.

Choosing Your Destiny
375 Pages

Most people leave their destiny to "chance." Whatever their parents happen to believe, they believe. This book shows that our "destiny" is God's most precious gift to us. Should we throw this gift to the wind? Should we allow "chance" rather than "choice" determine our destiny?

The Bahá'í Faith has come to give us spiritual insight and to help us choose our destiny in the light of reason and true knowledge, rather than in the darkness of tradition and conformity. The knowledge contained in *Choosing Your Destiny* can liberate us from past prejudices and illusions and set our souls free. It can help us become spiritual by developing "the divine image" in our soul.

One God, Many Faiths; One Garden, Many Flowers
290 Pages

One God, Many Faiths; One Garden, Many Flowers shows that in God's garden there are many fragrant flowers, planted and nourished by the same Gardener. The Bahá'í Faith has come to help us recognize the beauty of the garden, the harmony of the flowers, and the oneness of the Gardener.

When we realize that we are all one people, on one planet, under one God, with one common destiny, the walls of prejudice that divide God's beautiful garden will crumble. Only true knowledge and love can reveal this beauty and bring about this wonder. The Bahá'í Faith is that knowledge and that love. It penetrates the hearts and souls of humankind to dispel all shadows of prejudice and separation. It connects our hearts and reveals the beauty and splendor of our souls in the light of oneness. *One God, Many Faiths, One Garden, Many Flowers* offers you the knowledge that can change your destiny.

The Afterlife

Unto God Shall We Return
164 pages

This is a compilation from the Bahá'í Scriptures on the afterlife. It brings together the Writings of Bahá'u'lláh, the Báb, and 'Abdu'l-Bahá on the purpose of human life and the continuation of that purpose into the mysterious realms beyond. *Unto God Shall We Return* is compiled and arranged to portray a clear vision of the meaning of life—both here and hereafter—and to offer guidance about how we can prepare our soul for God's "many mansions in heaven."

A Messenger of Joy
112 Pages

A Messenger of Joy is the most comforting and positive book ever written on death and the afterlife. In consoling and uplifting the souls of the grieving, it sets a standard that is not likely to be surpassed for a long time.

This book portrays death as a message of joy and hope, and not as the news of sorrow and despair. It lifts the veil to show that death is not the end of life, but the beginning of an everlasting and most glorious journey toward God.

A Glimpse of Paradise

A Near-Death Vision
of the Next Life

This DVD (also video) contains a talk given by Reinee Pasarow about one of her near death visions. This is a state in which the individual shows no vital signs of life, yet experiences life to its fullest. What makes this story unique is this: Reinee's vision guided her to become a Bahá'í. She was given several clues by a spiritual being about the Bahá'í Faith. For instance, one of the titles of Bahá'u'lláh— the Blessed Beauty—was revealed to her. She was also told the word "justice" and shown the seat of the Universal House of Justice, exactly as it is built. Reinee had many unusual dreams as a child, and three near death visions.

We have added an introduction and a conclusion to this DVD to make it more attractive and meaningful to all viewers, especially to seekers. The introduction and conclusion present Biblical and Bahá'í references to the many clues that Mrs. Pasarow received while in the presence of the Being of Light.

Forthcoming Books

The Glory of the Son

It is absolutely essential to know why we believe in Jesus. Where can we find the answer? Only in the Words of Jesus Himself. *The Glory of the Son* offers a brief summary of all the reasons Jesus—not His followers—gave to substantiate His claim. This is a book that every Christian should read. It will also be of great value to those of the Jewish faith who have a desire to know the evidence for their glorious King and Redeemer: Jesus Christ.

Will Jesus Come from the Sky or as a Thief?

Be always on the watch! *Luke 21:36*

The day of the Lord will come like a thief in the night. *I Thess. 5:2*

In the mid-19th century many Christian scholars had discovered that, according to numerous biblical prophecies and promises, Christ would return in 1844. Thousands of Christians around the world expected His Return in that year. Why did so many discover the same date? And what piece of "the prophetic puzzle" did they miss? Let us explore this critical question.

Jesus declared that He would return "*like a thief.*" He also repeatedly warned us to "*Watch!*" How does a thief come? Secretly. A thief does not want to draw attention to himself. This is his foremost concern. How can we catch a thief? By being awake and "*watchful,*" by "*paying attention*" to his coming. Jesus' warning that He would return "*like a thief,*" and His recommended strategy for recognizing Him by staying *awake* and by "*watching*" for Him, are complementary:

The warning: I shall come like a thief!

The way to recognize me: Watch, pay close attention! Do not be complacent!

What, then, did Jesus mean by warning us repeatedly and emphatically to "*Watch!*"? He meant: "*Pay close attention to the news of My coming!*"

How did Jesus come the first time? Like a thief. He walked among the Jews. He knew every one of them, but with a few exceptions, they did not know Him. Jesus concealed His supreme glory from "the strangers," from all those who were unworthy of seeing the Spirit of God in Him (John 12:40), from all those who "*may look and look but see nothing*" (Mark 10:12). *Only the spiritually-sighted paid close attention to Him*, only they "watched" with their hearts and souls, and only they saw the glory of God in Him. Jesus did not allow the spiritually blind to witness His divine glory.

By the vivid expression "*like a thief*" Jesus instructs us to expect a repetition of the way He came the first time. He further confirms this fact by predicting that *people will respond to the News of His coming the same way that they responded to the News of the coming of Noah*. They will be complacent, non-attentive, negligent, and spiritually asleep!

What piece of "the prophetic puzzle" did Christians (who expected the Return of Christ in 1844) miss? The same "piece" that the Jews had missed 18 centuries earlier and are still missing! That piece is the word "*SPIRIT:*"

The "missing piece" for Jews:

He will come as a "*king*" means: "*His Spirit* will come as a king."

The "missing piece" for Christians:

He will come from *heaven* means: "*His Spirit* will come from heaven."

Jesus Himself decoded the word "sky" or "heaven" several times. Compare the following two verses, one from *Jesus Christ, the Anointed One of God*; the other from *Bahá'u'lláh, the Glory of God*:

I [the Spirit of God, Christ] have come down from heaven.   *Christ (John 6:38)*

He [the Spirit of God, Bahá'u'lláh], verily, hath again come down from heaven, even as He came down from it the first time.
                    Bahá'u'lláh (the Glory of God)

Muhammad: the Spirit Who Glorified Jesus

This book introduces Islam from a Bahá'í perspective. It demonstrates a remarkable harmony between the Bible and the Qur'án. It also responds to the objections raised against Islam.

Does Your Fish Bowl Need Fresh Water?

This book is written to refresh the life of the soul. Its prime purpose is to advance the "knowledge of God," so that we may know our Creator as He really is, not as we may wish Him to be!

A poet once said: "God is closer to me than I am to myself. Why, then, am I so far from Him?" How can this be possible? The distance between our spirit and the Spirit of God can be measured by the difference between God as He really is, and the God that we have created in our mind. The purpose of acquiring the "knowledge of God" is to diminish the distance. The more we know God as He really is, the closer we draw to Him.

Our purpose in coming to this world is spiritual transformation, which can be attained only by knowing and loving God. *Does Your Fish Bowl Need Fresh Water?* will help you attain this Most Glorious Purpose. It appeals both to the mind and to the heart. It satisfies the mind by presenting the latest scientific evidence for the existence of God and the afterlife. It inspires and transforms the heart by showing the everlasting honors and rewards in store for those who cultivate their spiritual potential and the unimaginable losses for those who fail in this endeavor.

How would you feel if you traveled for 70 years toward a destination, and then at the end of this journey, you suddenly discovered that you had traveled in the wrong direction? This is the way many people squander the precious days of their lives. Imagine their disappointment at the end of their spiritual journey! Should we not then learn a lesson from their lives? Should we not take a little time for our soul while we still have a chance?

Appendix

A Letter for New Seekers

The following is a copy of a letter that I give to many of those with whom I share the news of the Advent of Bahá'u'lláh. Please feel free to reproduce copies.

> Brighten our hearts, O my Lord, with the splendor of Thy knowledge, and illumine our sight with the light of such eyes as are fixed upon the horizon of Thy grace and the Day-Spring of Thy glory.[1]   Bahá'u'lláh

Dear Friend:

You should feel honored to be among those who have heard the news of the Advent of Bahá'u'lláh, the Glory of God. I pray that your knowledge will lead you to His Presence. The first requirement for success is removing "the veils of idle fancies" or "unverified and false assumptions" that surround us:

> …free thyself from *the veils of idle fancies* and enter into My court, that thou mayest be fit for everlasting life and worthy to meet Me.[2]   Bahá'u'lláh

Only by removing "the veils" can the light of knowledge reach us and lead us to *true faith.* Only then can we attain the honor of *seeing the glory of God.*

> Did I not tell you that if you have *faith,* you will *see the glory of God*?"
>   Christ (John 11:40 NB)

Prophecies declare that among the many who are "called" only *a few* will succeed in freeing their souls from "the veils." Only *a few* will be able to join the ranks of the ones chosen by God:

> ...*many* are called, but *few* chosen.
>> Christ (Matt. 20:16 NKJ)

In this letter I wish to share with you some insight about the choices you will make. Over the years I have noticed that those who are called to know Bahá'u'lláh fall into one of these groups:

- Many of them fail to investigate His message beyond their first exposure.

- Some of them investigate His message for a while—perhaps for a few weeks or months—and then stop.

- A few of them continue their investigation until they arrive at a conclusion.

Do you belong to the first, the second, or the third group? You will soon discover for yourself. You have, of course, full freedom to join the ranks of any group that you wish. I hope and pray that you will choose to join the ranks of the third group by continuing your investigation. To help you make the best choice, let me remind you of a universal law found in all the sacred Scriptures. It is *the*

Law of Reciprocity. According to this Law, God will treat us the way we treat Him:

> *For with the same measure that you use, it will be measured back to you.*
> *Christ (Luke 6:38 ✻)*

Let us now apply *the Law of Reciprocity* to the consequence of accepting or rejecting God's invitation to investigate the news of the Advent of His great Messengers and Redeemers. Only God has the authority to set these laws, to speak in this language, and to give such warnings:

> But he who denies Me before men will be denied before the angels of God.
> Christ (Luke 12:9)

> God will verily do unto them that which they themselves are doing, and will forget them even as they have ignored His Presence in His day. Such is His decree unto those that have denied Him, and such will it be unto them that have rejected His signs.[3]   Bahá'u'lláh

Recognition of *the Law of Reciprocity* will empower our soul with "fear of God"—an

165

awareness of His awesome authority—and then it will lead us to wisdom, the most precious of all virtues:

> The fear of the Lord is the beginning of wisdom…   Psalms 111:10

> The essence of wisdom is the fear of God…and the apprehension of His justice and decree.[4]   Bahá'u'lláh

Hearing about the News of the Advent of Bahá'u'lláh not only offers you a chance to attain the greatest glory and honor, it also places a special responsibility on your conscience. This is because after you hear the News, a second law takes effect. It is *the Law of Justice*, expressed in these words:

> *From everyone who has been given much, much will be demanded*; and from the one who has been entrusted with much, much more will be asked.
>   Christ (Luke 12:48 NIV)

This letter expresses my love for all those seekers with whom I share this Greatest and most Glorious News: the Advent of the Glory of God—the One for whom the world has been awaiting for thousands of years. Its purpose is to help you recognize the great honor of hearing about Bahá'u'lláh and the heavenly fruits that this knowledge can bear for you for all eternity. I hope and pray that you will make every effort to join the third group by responding positively—with all your heart and soul—to God's invitation to investigate the news of the Advent of His new Messenger and Redeemer, Bahá'u'lláh, the Glory of God.

My experience shows that almost all people are quite busy. If that is a good reason for ignoring this News, then where can we find those who will investigate this News? Should we look for them in outer space? Devoting even as little as ten minutes a day will allow you to join the third group. Even five minutes a day may keep the flame of your search alive, and would show your devotion to God and to what He has planned for you.

If your car starts one out of three times, do you consider it faithful?

If you fail to come to work two or three times a month, does your boss call you faithful?

If your water heater greets you with cold water once in a while, do you call it faithful?

If you miss a couple of mortgage payments a year, does the loan company say, "Oh, well, 10 out of 12 is not too bad"?

If we expect faithfulness from other people and things, does not God expect the same—if not more—from us?

If at this point in your life, even five minutes a day is too much for you to devote to your everlasting destiny, then you may wish to keep this letter as a reminder to do in the future what you cannot do now.

May God give you plenty of time to investigate the news of the Advent of Bahá'u'lláh—the most awesome revelation of Knowledge from God—before your share of time has come to an end. May God bless you and aid you in all your endeavors.

Magnified be Thy name, O Lord my God! Thou art He Whom all things worship and Who worshipeth no one… I implore Thee…to enable me to drink deep of the living waters through which

Thou hast vivified the hearts of Thy chosen ones and quickened the souls of them that love Thee, that I may, at all times and under all conditions, turn my face wholly towards Thee.

Thou art the God of power, of glory and bounty. No God is there beside Thee, the Supreme Ruler, the All-Glorious, the Omniscient.[5] Bahá'u'lláh

With loving greetings,

Hugh Motlagh

References

Unto God Shall We Return

1. *Selections from the Writings of the Báb*, p. 9.
2. *The Kitáb-i-Íqán*, p. 90.
3. *The Hidden Words of Bahá'u'lláh* (Arabic), no. 32.
4. *The Hidden Words of Bahá'u'lláh* (Arabic), no. 34.
5. *The Promulgation of Universal Peace*, p. 214.
6. Rabbání, Rúhíyyih. *Prescription for Living*, Oxford: George Ronald, 1978, p. 93.
7. *The Hidden Words of Bahá'u'lláh* (Persian), no. 19.
8. Dyer, Wayne W. *You'll See It When You Believe It*, New York: Avon Books, 1989, p. 15.
9. *The Hidden Words of Bahá'u'lláh* (Arabic), no. 14.
10. *The Kitáb-i-Íqán*, p. 101.
11. *Gleanings from the Writings of Bahá'u'lláh*, p.158.
12. Attributed to John Bigelow.
13. *Tablets of Bahá'u'lláh*, pp. 187-188.

14. Wernher Von Braun.

15. Moody, Raymond, Jr. *Light Beyond*, New York: Bantam Books, 1989, p. 171.

16. Moody, Raymond, Jr. *Light Beyond*, New York: Bantam Books, 1989, p. 172.

17. A. J. Cronin.

18. Johann Wolfgang von Goethe.

19. Juliette Adam.

20. *Prayers and Meditations by Bahá'u'lláh*, p. 209.

21. *Tablets of Bahá'u'lláh,* p. 232.

22. Moody, Raymond, Jr. *Light Beyond*, New York: Bantam Books, 1989, pp. 75-76.

23. Moody, Raymond, Jr. *Light Beyond*, New York: Bantam Books, 1989, p. 198.

24. *Tablets of Bahá'u'lláh,* p. 189.

25. *The Seven Valleys and the Four Valleys*, p. 58.

26. *Epistle to the Son of the Wolf*, p. 107.

27. *The Hidden Words of Bahá'u'lláh* (Arabic), no. 55.

28. *The Compilation of Compilations*, Volume II, p. 379.

29. *Tablets of Bahá'u'lláh,* p. 155.

30. *Gleanings from the Writings of Bahá'u'lláh*, pp. 155-157.

31. Paul Speicher.

32. *Gleanings from the Writings of Bahá'u'lláh*, p. 150.

33. Moody, Raymond, Jr. *Light Beyond*, New York: Bantam Books, 1989, p. 48.

34. *The Hidden Words of Bahá'u'lláh* (Persian), no. 59.

35. Rúhíyyih Rabbání. *Prescription for Living*, Oford: George Ronald, 1978, pp. 101-103.

36. Stephen Ben.

37. The Talmud.

38. *Gleanings from the Writings of Bahá'u'lláh*, p. 34.

39. *The Hidden Words of Bahá'u'lláh* (Arabic), no. 63.

40. Tryon Edwards.

41. Rúhíyyih Rabbání. *Prescription fro Living*, Oxford: George Ronald, 1978, p. 101.

42. Henry Beecher.

43. Ed Howe.

44. *The Hidden Words of Bahá'u'lláh* (Persian), no. 27.

45. *Tablets of Bahá'u'lláh,* p. 189.

46. *Selections from the Writings of the Báb*, pp. 88-89.

47. *Selections from the Writings of 'Abdu'l-Bahá*, p. 201.

48. *Selections from the Writings of 'Abdu'l-Bahá*, p. 239.

49. *The Hidden Words of Bahá'u'lláh* (Persian), no. 40.

50. *The Hidden Words of Bahá'u'lláh* (Arabic), no. 33.

51. Moody, Raymond, Jr. *The Light Beyond*, New York: Bantam Books, 1989, p. 100.

52. Samuel Lindsay.

53. Henry Van Dyke.

54. Josh Billings.

55. William James.

56. *Tablets of Bahá'u'lláh,* p. 172.

57. Rúhíyyih Rabbání. *Prescription fro Living*, Oxford: George Ronald, 1978, p. 95.

58. Etienne de Grallet.

59. Thomas Carlyle.

60. Rúhíyyih Rabbání. *Prescription fro Living*, Oxford: George Ronald, 1978, pp. 96-97.

61. *Gleanings from the Writings of Bahá'u'lláh*, p. 261.

62. *Gleanings from the Writings of Bahá'u'lláh*, p. 125.
63. *The Kitáb-i-Íqán*, p. 24.
64. *Gleanings from the Writings of Bahá'u'lláh*, p. 206.
65. *The Proclamation of Bahá'u'lláh*, p. 96.
66. *The Promulgation of Universal Peace*, p. 226.
67. *Selections from the Writings of the Báb*, p. 80.
68. *The Hidden Words of Bahá'u'lláh* (Arabic), no. 1.
69. *The Kitáb-i-Íqán*, p. 3.
70. *The Hidden Words of Bahá'u'lláh* (Persian), no. 69.
71. *Gleanings from the Writings of Bahá'u'lláh*, p. 178.
72. *Tablets of Bahá'u'lláh,* p. 86.
73. *The Hidden Words of Bahá'u'lláh* (Persian), no. 75.
74. *Epistle to the Son of the Wolf*, p. 49.
75. *The Hidden Words of Bahá'u'lláh* (Arabic), no. 3.
76. Paul Devies.
77. Charlotte Cushman.
78. *The Kitáb-i-Íqán*, pp. 8-9.
79. *Gleanings from the Writings of Bahá'u'lláh*, p. 149.
80. *Some Answered Questions*, pp. 235-236.
81. *Gleanings from the Writings of Bahá'u'lláh*, p. 70.
82. Megiddo Message.
83. *Selections from the Writings of the Báb*, p. 121.
84. *Tablets of Bahá'u'lláh*, p. 156.
85. *Gleanings from the Writings of Bahá'u'lláh*, p. 68.
86. George W. Truett.
87. *The Hidden Words of Bahá'u'lláh* (Arabic), no. 23.
88. *The Hidden Words of Bahá'u'lláh* (Persian), no. 37.
89. *The Hidden Words of Bahá'u'lláh* (Persian), no. 75.
90. *The Kitáb-i-Íqán*, p. 252.
91. *Selections from the Writings of the Báb*, p. 89.

92. *Gleanings from the Writings of Bahá'u'lláh*, p. 262.
93. *The Hidden Words of Bahá'u'lláh* (Persian), no. 40.
94. *Tablets of Bahá'u'lláh*, p. 138.
95. *Gleanings from the Writings of Bahá'u'lláh*, p. 94.

Quotations from Sacred Scriptures

1. *The Hidden Words of Bahá'u'lláh* (Arabic), no. 6.
2. *Gleanings from the Writings of Bahá'u'lláh*, p. 345.
3. *Gleanings from the Writings of Bahá'u'lláh*, pp. 345-346.
4. *Gleanings from the Writings of Bahá'u'lláh*, p. 161.
5. *The Hidden Words of Bahá'u'lláh* (Arabic), no. 31.
6. *Gleanings from the Writings of Bahá'u'lláh*, p. 328.
7. *Gleanings from the Writings of Bahá'u'lláh*, pp. 328-329.
8. *The Hidden Words of Bahá'u'lláh* (Arabic), no. 55.
9. *The Hidden Words of Bahá'u'lláh* (Persian), no. 14.
10. *Gleanings from the Writings of Bahá'u'lláh*, p. 127.
11. *The Kitáb-i-Íqán*, p. 24.
12. *Selections from the Writings of the Báb*, p. 158.
13. *Selections from the Writings of the Báb*, p. 103.
14. *Paris Talks*, p. 85.
15. *Selections from the Writings of 'Abdu'l-Bahá*, p. 3.
16. *The Hidden Words of Bahá'u'lláh* (Persian), no. 73.
17. *Gleanings from the Writings of Bahá'u'lláh*, pp. 326-327.
18. *The Dawn-Breakers, New York*: Bahá'í Publishing Committee, 1953, p. 94.
19. *Paris Talks*, p. 166.
20. *Gleanings from the Writings of Bahá'u'lláh*, p. 299.

21. *Gleanings from the Writings of Bahá'u'lláh*, p. 70.

22. *Gleanings from the Writings of Bahá'u'lláh*, p. 68.

23. *Gleanings from the Writings of Bahá'u'lláh*, p. 71.

24. *Gleanings from the Writings of Bahá'u'lláh*, p. 157.

25. *Tablets of Bahá'u'lláh*, p. 113.

26. *Selections from the Writings of the Báb*, p. 165.

27. *Selections from the Writings of the Báb*, p. 117.

28. *Paris Talks*, p. 122.

29. *Paris Talks*, p. 113.

30. *Paris Talks*, p. 177.

31. *The Promulgation of Universal Peace*, p. 335.

32. *The Promulgation of Universal Peace*, p. 335.

Prayers

1. *Prayers and Meditations by Bahá'u'lláh*, pp. 261-262.

2. *Gleanings from the Writings of Bahá'u'lláh*, pp. 133-134.

3. *Bahá'í Prayers*, Wilmette, IL: Bahá'í Publishing Trust, 1991 edition, pp. 43-45.

4. *Selections from the Writings of the Báb*, pp. 203-204.

5. *Selections from the Writings of the Báb*, p. 177.

6. *Selections from the Writings of the Báb*, p. 210.

7. *Selections from the Writings of the Báb*, p. 182.

8. *Selections from the Writings of the Báb*, p. 178.

9. *Selections from the Writings of the Báb*, p. 177.

10. *Bahá'í Prayers*, Wilmette, IL: Bahá'í Publishing Trust, 1991 edition, pp. 45-46.

11. *Selections from the Writings of 'Abdu'l-Bahá*, pp. 196-197.

12. *Bahá'í Prayers*, Wilmette, IL: Bahá'í Publishing Trust, 2002 edition, p. 35.

13. *Synopsis and Codification of the Laws and Ordinances of the the Kitáb-i-Aqdas*, p. 62.

14. *Bahá'í Prayers*, Wilmette, IL: Bahá'í Publishing Trust, 2002 edition, pp. 35-36.

Unto God Shall We Return
164 Pages, $6.00

Selections from the Bahá'í Scriptures on the Afterlife

This is the most reliable and comprehensive source of information on the destiny, reality, and immortality of the human soul.

Unto God Shall We Return portrays a most glorious destiny for those who fulfill their lives' purpose during their short stay on this planet. It shows that death is not a voyage to grave, but to God. This book brings comfort to all those who mourn the loss of their loved ones, and instills hope, peace, and joy by unveiling glimpses of the glories that await anyone who fulfills his mission on earth and joins the host of heaven.

We are not permanent residents of this planet, but travelers on a journey to a new and exciting world:

> O Son of Man! Sorrow not save that thou art far from Us. Rejoice not save that thou art drawing near and returning unto Us.
> Bahá'u'lláh

> Man is the life of the world, and the life of man is the spirit...Rejoice, for the life eternal is awaiting you.
> 'Abdu'l-Bahá

A Website to Help You Cultivate Your Spiritual Potential

www.globalperspective.org

This Website is designed to serve the followers of all religions and those of no religion. Its message is universal and relevant to all ages, especially young people in search of a meaning and an enduring purpose in life. It can assist you in the following ways:

- Help you choose your everlasting destiny in the light of knowledge and full awareness.

- Strengthen your faith and cultivate your spiritual potential.

- Help you find the means for creating a more pleasant and peaceful world.

- Offer you a global perspective on God's Plan for humankind expressed in the advent of many great religions throughout history, and in this age through the advent of the Bahá'í Faith.

On this Website you will find "Pamphlets" on many topics, which you can download and print for study and distribution.